THE MEASUREMENT OF VALUES

A Monograph in

MODERN CONCEPTS OF PHILOSOPHY

Series Editor

MARVIN FARBER

State University of New York at Buffalo
Buffalo, New York

Titles appearing in this series do not necessarily reflect the thinking of the author or publisher. The series has been developed to present *all* modern concepts of philosophy.

The following titles have either been published in the series or are in production and will be published soon.

THE
MEASUREMENT
OF VALUES

Behavorial Science and Philosophical Approaches

ROLLO HANDY

State University of New York at Buffalo
Buffalo, New York

WARREN H. GREEN, INC.

St. Louis, Missouri, U.S.A.

Published by

WARREN H. GREEN, INC.
10 South Brentwood Blvd.
St. Louis, Missouri 63105, U.S.A.

Library of Congress Catalog Card No. 79-110107

Printed in the United States of America
3-A   (177)

PREFACE

There is an extensive literature on values both in philosophy and in the behavioral sciences. Philosophers have often placed major emphasis on attempts to clarify value terminology and to differentiate values from the rest of the universe. Behavioral scientists have emphasized the description of the values held by particular individuals or groups of humans, and often have claimed to measure values. This book is the product of an effort to combine the relatively empirical work of behavioral scientists with the relatively theoretical work of philosophers, in the hope that a more adequate understanding of what is involved in value measurement will result.

Much of the research for this volume was completed in the 1967-1968 academic year, while I was on a sabbatical leave spent at the University of California in Berkeley. I am indebted to the State University of New York at Buffalo for the sabbatical, to the Research Foundation of State University of New York for a research fellowship granted me during that period, to my hosts at Berkeley, and to the Progress Foundation for a more recent research grant. I also would like to express appreciation to my wife, Toni, for her helpful criticism of the content of this book and her valiant (if sometimes unsuccessful) efforts to make my writing clearer and less pedantic.

R. H.

121.8
H192 m

CONTENTS

THE MEASUREMENT OF VALUES

Chapter I

INTRODUCTION

A. AIM OF BOOK

The title of this book probably will suggest different themes to various readers. Some may expect to find the development of a particular metric suitable for values; some a treatment of the problems associated with the measurement of subjective entities such as utility; some the construction of formal models for value decision situations; and yet others may expect a critical survey of behavioral science inquiries purporting to measure values.

A major reason many different expectations are generated by the phrase 'measurement of values' is that there are so many conflicting notions of how 'value' is best used.[1] Given some uses of 'value,' the measurement of values in almost any plausible sense is either theoretically impossible or extremely difficult; given other uses, there may be few theoretical problems but serious practical or laboratory difficulties. There are also important disagreements about the nature of measurement and its applicability to some aspects of human behavior.

In view of such disagreements, one expects to find the literature on value measurement encompassing many topics and that investigations apparently of the same or similar topics are actually about quite different matters. In such a situation, a tempting strategy is to begin with a preferred use of 'value,' and then de-

---

[1] For a discussion of this issue in some detail, see Rollo Handy, *Value Theory and the Behavioral Sciences*, Springfield, Charles C Thomas, 1969, Chs. 2 and 3.

velop a suitable methodology for inquiring into values as thus viewed.[2] A particular mode, or several modes, of measurement would then be appropriate, and the focus of attention could be almost exclusively on the problems and potentialities of measurement within the chosen framework.

That approach has much to commend it, but there are also drawbacks. For one thing, as Hull notes, the great diversity of attempted specifications of 'value' is a prominent feature of the field, and unless one accepts the use of 'value' suggested by a given author, much of what he says about measurement will be beside the point. In addition, the consequences for measurement that follow from any particular approach to value can be useful evidence in the selection of the most adequate use of 'value.'

Another general approach is to look in detail at the attempts of behavioral scientists to measure values, and then see what the difficulties are, what the successes are, and what implications may be drawn as to the most effective use of 'value.' A difficulty is that often accounts of purported measurements of value either do not tell us clearly how 'value' is used in the inquiry, or the use adopted is so restricted that the results are not very illuminating.

In this book, elements of both the general approaches just mentioned will be used. Considerable attention will be given to the work of both behavioral scientists and philosophers on value measurement, and attention will also be focused on a proposed value theory that seems to offer many advantages. A major group of opponents against which this book is directed consists of those who maintain that values in principle cannot be measured and that any attempt to measure them is a denigration of values or a badly misdirected effort.

In my opinion one can hardly overemphasize the amount of disagreement found in the literature bearing on value measurement, for there are not only diverse views on what measurement in general is, and what values in general are, but also on what scientific method is. To illustrate, I want to quote briefly from both an economist and a psychologist.

---

[2]This is the approach, for example, of Clark L. Hull in his "Value, Valuation, and Natural-Science Methodology," *Philosophy of Science*, Vol. 11, 1944.

Lionel Robbins held a point of view that is still encountered in one way or another:

"Scientific method, it is urged, demands that we should leave out of account anything which is incapable of direct observation. . . . Valuation is a subjective process. We cannot *observe* valuation. It is therefore out of place in a scientific explanation. Our theoretical constructions must assume observable data. . . . The argument that we should do nothing that is not done in the physical sciences is very seductive. But . . . . our business is to explain certain aspects of conduct. And it is very questionable whether this can be done in terms which involve no psychical element. It is quite certain that. . . . we do in fact *understand* terms such as choice, indifference, preference, and the like in terms of inner experience. The idea of an end, which is fundamental to our conception of the economic, is not possible to define in terms of external behaviour only. If we are to explain the relationships which arise from the existence of a scarcity of means in relation to a multiplicity of ends, surely at least one-half of the equation, as it were, must be psychical in character. . . . It is really not possible to understand the concepts of choice, of the relationship of means and ends, the central concepts of our science, in terms of observation of external data."[3]

The passage just quoted exemplifies a number of beliefs and assumptions that have been challenged by other workers. For example, many would deny that scientists are restricted to "direct" observation and would want to include "indirect" observation at the very least. Some would maintain that valuations are as observable as many other forms of human behavior, and deny that valuations are less "objective" than many other processes or events inquired into by scientists. Some would object to the restriction of scientific inquiry to "external" behavior, and indeed reject the conventional internal-external dichotomy in attempts to describe human behavior. The apparent coupling of "understanding" with "psychical" entities would be rejected by many workers. The exclusion of purposive processes from what can

---

[3]Lionel Robbins, *An Essay on the Nature and Significance of Economic Science*, 2nd ed., London, Macmillan, 1935, pp. 87-90.

be inquired into by the procedures of the physical sciences also would be challenged by many.[4]

L. L. Thurstone takes a position that in some ways is strongly opposed to Robbins' view. He begins by mentioning that some of his colleagues in the humanities shudder at the idea of measuring values, maintain that attitudes contain some essence that simply cannot be adequately identified and measured, and hold that any attempt to do so would only produce measurements of the trivial. Thurstone rejects all that, but goes on to say:

> "Human values are essentially subjective. They can certainly not be adequately represented by physical objects. Their intensities or magnitudes cannot be represented by physical measurement. At the very start we are faced with the problem of establishing a subjective metric. This is the central theme in modern psychophysics in its many applications to the measurement of social values, moral values, and esthetic values. Exactly the same problem reappears in the measurement of utility in economics."[5]

Although in my opinion many of the specific problems Thurstone considers need to be taken account of in any scientific attempt to measure values, those who agree with him on such topics still could deny that values are "subjective," and could question the usefulness of the subjective-objective distinction in that context. Without being told more precisely what values are, we cannot say to what extent they can or cannot be represented by physical measurements. In short, the apparent dualism between the "subjective" and the "physical" accepted here by Thurstone would be challenged by many who agree with him that values can be measured. As often happens, we are enmeshed not only in

---

[4]The network of issues here is complicated. My views on those issues can be found in detail in Rollo Handy and Paul Kurtz, *A Current Appraisal of the Behavioral Sciences*, Great Barrington, Behavioral Research Council, 1964; Rollo Handy, *Methodology of the Behavioral Sciences*, Springfield, Charles C Thomas, 1964; and in Rollo Handy and E. C. Harwood, "Trial Names," in Alfred de Grazia, Rollo Handy, E. C. Harwood, and Paul Kurtz, eds., *The Behavioral Sciences: Essays in Honor of George A. Lundberg*, Great Barrington, Behavioral Research Council, 1968.

[5]L. L. Thurstone, "The Measurement of Values," *Psychological Review*, Vol. 61, 1954, p. 47.

questions about technical problems of measurement, but about what human behavior is and how best to inquire into it.

In addition to the type of controversy just discussed, there are also controversies as to the adequacy of most measurements in the behavioral sciences, so that even if valuations are regarded as nonmysterious forms of behavior there still can be many disputes about the possibility and adequacy of measuring them. Such differences of opinion are not surprising, and I am not claiming that the field of value measurement is characterized by worse disagreement than many other fields of inquiry. The moral I do draw is that work on value measurement should not overlook any of the areas of disagreement mentioned or pretend they are not there.

Further, I think it is often extremely dangerous to proceed as if some one area of inquiry were well enough established so that one could uncritically accept conclusions there as a foundation for further work. In the present instance, for example, I believe it would be unwise to assume that any available theory of measurement is necessarily fully acceptable. In general, any mode of inquiry should always be open to modification (including rejection) on the basis both of the results achieved by using that mode of inquiry and also of other warranted information that becomes available. The hope of finding some elemental building blocks that are guaranteed useful for all further inquiry is not only historically suspect, it may serve to impede inquiry just where it is most needed. The whole of this book, then, is regarded as tentative, provisional, and subject to change. Not only is finality rejected, my hope is that improvements will be necessitated immediately, for progress consists not in reaching some theoretically indubitable conclusions, but in improving the reliability, adequacy, etc., of the results of our inquiries.

B. SCIENTIFIC INQUIRY

So many of the disagreements about the central concerns of this book involve differing views on the nature of scientific inquiry that it seems appropriate to consider some aspects of scientific inquiry in the first chapter. The number of controversies about scientific method, and the many shades of opinion that can be found, are so great that no detailed discussion will be attempted here. Instead the general point of view adopted will be described in enough detail so that those who disagree can locate their differences with reasonable adequacy. The view described here stems from an attempt to look at the history of science in order to ascertain both the method used in some of the most successful of such inquiries and to see why some of the "blind alleys" were not productive.

No assertion is made here that scientific method is completely developed, for in my view it definitely is still in the making. Thus the basic problem is not to find the best description for a completed process; presumably more adequate descriptions of even its present stage will be developed in the future. The self-correcting character of scientific inquiry and the tentativeness of the results gained through that inquiry deserve strong emphasis; the "quest for certainty" is abjured. Indeed, on the view adopted here, a main characteristic of scientific inquiry is the search for ever higher probability than previously attained without expecting certainty. All statements in scientific inquiry, from the most elementary observations of data to the most general conclusions, are subject to possible modification, correction, or rejection.

On the other hand, the skepticism of received results, opinions, techniques, presuppositions, theories, etc., in scientific inquiry should not be understood as a support of "subjectivity" or as leading to a chaotic clash of opinions. The high degree of agreement reached by scientists following the same procedures is noteworthy in contemporary civilization, and is in marked contrast to the differences in conclusions generated by many other methods. The disavowal of the "quest for certainty" helps, then, to foster a certain type of agreement rather than contributing to a conflict of views. Methods of resolving scientific differences that are shared by all the participants in a controversy are often available, and the results of scientific inquiries frequently are cumulative. The persistent unresolved issues usually stem from theoretical differences for which adequate testing procedures are not yet available, situations in which the accumulated data are not decisive for resolving the difference, or from terminological confusion.

Lest the foregoing be misunderstood, there is no assumption here that scientists are better, more intelligent, or more diligent than other humans. Nor is the key merely that scientists tend to accept certain principles by means of which disagreements can be resolved. Those accepting the same religious dogma, for example, are likely to reach the same conclusions about many matters within a given theological context. To the extent that there is a key, it seems to be that the accepted methods within scientific inquiry are such as to produce reliable predictive techniques and (often) reliable control of events that are humanly important.

The usefulness of scientific inquiry, then, is indicated by the extent to which its results facilitate prediction and control (and/or adjustive behavior). A hypothesis that later is superseded by a better one still may yield useful predictions; the mere occurrence of some successful predictions does not imply that a particular hypothesis is final or will not later be improved upon or rejected. The self-corrective character of scientific inquiry results in hypotheses being modified or abandoned when their predictions fail, assuming that we have reasonably adequate ways of measuring the success or failure of the relevant predictions.

'Control' has a pejorative connotation for many these days, for they feel uninhibited or "unleashed" scientific inquiry may diminish their freedom or turn men into robots. In general, the more highly warranted information we have, the greater the possibility that such information will be used in a fashion detrimental to someone. But by the same token, the more highly warranted information we have, the greater the possibility that we can improve human welfare. A person who is not aware of the existence of aspirin and has none available is not going to die of aspirin poisoning, but is also likely to suffer many unnecessary aches and pains. In any event, when reliable information about human behavior is discovered, one's freedom may be expanded rather than diminished, even if other people find ways of influencing one's behavior that were not previously available.

We presumably do not feel that our freedom is threatened or diminished when inquiry into a disease is followed by its control and near-abolition. Most often, or at least frequently, those who object to "control" point to some of the untoward technological results made possible by scientific inquiry. Again, let me emphasize that I am not at all denying that many highly undesirable consequences can flow from the discovery of new warranted assertions, but I suggest that rather than romantically bemoaning those consequences, we need further information that will help us decrease the undesired results and increase the desired results.

Few who are alarmed about our increasing ability to predict would actually want to turn the clock back if that were possible. This becomes more evident if we keep in mind the many benefits prediction allows even where direct control is not possible; for example, being able to predict which mushrooms are edible enables those who have such information to adjust their behavior favorably even if we cannot now control the effects of eating some poisonous mushrooms. So it is not the general level of prediction and control made possible through successful scientific inquiry that is objected to, but rather that *some* consequences of applied scientific findings are not wanted. The remedy seems to be more scientific inquiry, not less; i.e., a better understanding of human behavior to go along with our increased understanding in the physical and physiological sciences.

As suggested in the foregoing, the view of scientific method adopted here relies on a close relation between the development of theory and the collection of data. Hypotheses may be generated in a wide variety of ways, but since hypotheses are developed in order to account for some set of data, they are usually developed from a consideration of that data. They are controlled by the data in the sense of being accepted, modified, or abandoned on the basis of the best available information. Neither the data that lead to the formulation of a hypothesis nor those that test it are fixed once and for all. Better techniques of observation and measurement may result in radical changes in what once were taken to be indisputable facts. Further, the development of highly warranted hypotheses may enable us to measure or observe data much more adequately than previously was possible, and in that sense theory helps to establish facts.

None of the above, of course, is to be understood as ruling out the development of hypotheses ranging far beyond any data available at the moment, or the collection of data that presently do not seem relevant to any existing hypotheses, or a division of labor between the theoretician and the laboratorian. Rather, what is urged here is that in successful scientific inquiries there often is both an elaborate testing of hypotheses and the development of new hypotheses that further our understanding of available data. This kind of union of theory and practice seems to offer the maximum opportunity for correcting presumed facts in the light of well-supported generalizations and for minimizing the time and effort spent on hypotheses that are badly out of accord with experimental findings.

In harmony with this "open-ended" approach, Dewey's term 'warranted assertion' is preferred to 'law,' 'truth,' etc., in order to focus attention on the corrigibility of all aspects of scientific inquiry. The use of 'warranted assertion' may help discourage the view that science has discovered, or will discover, final, fixed, or indubitable generalizations. It also may be useful in reminding us that the assertion in question is warranted by a definite process of inquiry, which is open to replication and subject to further improvement. A warranted assertion, then, with its ground, justification, or warrant open to inspection and criticism, and with its range of application specified, seems to be the immediate end product of successful scientific inquiries.

Implicit in some views of scientific method is a type of architectural view that is here opposed. Some accounts suggest that science develops in layers, so to speak (or can be thus arranged logically), in which cumulative additions to the store of facts are made and theories constructed on the basis of those facts. Although something like that often does happen, the oversimplification involved can be dangerous. The naivete of assuming there is a pure given in perception, or that we have complete knowledge of some hard facts upon which we can safely base our theories, is sometimes carried over into methodological discussions, and the critical scrutiny and constant rechecking of both data and theory are insufficiently emphasized. The methodology used should be as much under the control of well-supported findings as future research is under the control of a critically developed methodology.

At various stages in scientific inquiry, quite different levels of precision in quantification may be proper. On the one hand, some defenders of a "humanistic" behavioral science make a fetish of the "evils" of quantification and overlook the fact that often their own statements are quantified in a crude form (in their use of terms such as 'more,' 'less,' 'many,' 'some,' 'few'). The increased precision of measurement and the more adequate description of the relationships among things and events that result from successful quantification make quantifying desirable when possible. But to insist that assertions are warranted only if elaborately and precisely quantified neglects much of the history of science; often in an early stage of inquiry even crude quantification may be useful and mark an important advance. Precise quantification is not always needed for humanly significant prediction and control.

In the same spirit, the position adopted here does not require that warranted assertions have a high degree of generality; i.e., apply to a wide range of things and events. Some critics object to the existing results of behavioral science inquiries on the ground that they seldom if ever have the order of generality sometimes found in the physical sciences. Much of the successful work in the behavioral sciences begins with simple description and then proceeds to more systematic classification, including taxonomic ordering, statistical ordering, and evolutionary ordering in terms of stages of development. What level of generality is useful depends on the question asked. If, for example, we are interested in the kinship system and marriage patterns of the Iroquois, highly warranted scientific results will presumably refer to only a small fraction of humanity, but the fact that warranted assertions about the Iroquois are not applicable to all, most, or many other cultural groups does not detract from the scientific merits of those assertions.

The above account of scientific inquiry is much more "pragmatic" or "instrumentalist" than many other accounts that have been given by both practicing scientists and philosophers of science. Some workers still emphasize explanations of phenomena that are subjectively satisfying; many commentators in recent years have emphasized a highly formal approach; while yet others have little concern for the possible uses of scientific findings in the solution of human problems. The view defended here is only tentative, and is suggested because it seems in accord with much that is usually included in the history of science. As noted, the immediate purpose is not to defend or even state in full detail the view adopted, but only to give enough detail so that the present approach will be intelligible and its relation to the rest of the book clear.

The conclusions one reaches about the issues just discussed are important not only in ascertaining what is scientifically warranted, but in determining what research strategies are used for measuring values. To illustrate the latter point, the kind of formal models developed by some economists, game theorists, and decision theorists will be mentioned. In Chapter VI, I am highly critical of the use such workers make of *utility,* and argue that we do not know what aspects of behavior 'utility' refers to, that the postulates used in the models are either inconsistent with warranted information about behavior or that they have not been tested, etc. My arguments there stem from the view of scientific inquiry described earlier in this section.

Those defending formal models often take a quite different view. For example, although Luce and Raiffa regard utility theory as "an indispensable tool" for their book, they emphasize how difficult it is "to determine a person's utility function even under the most ideal and idealized experimental conditions," and add that "one can almost say that it has yet to be done." But nonetheless they argue work should continue on that topic. Their rationale follows:

"If it is so difficult to determine utility functions under the best of conditions, there is certainly no hope at all that it can be done under field conditions for situations of practical interest. Thus, if the theories built upon utility theory really demand such measurements, they are doomed practically; if they can be useful without making such measurements, then why go to the trouble of learning how? As in the physical sciences, we would claim that a theory may very well postulate quantities which cannot be measured in general, and yet that it will be possible to derive some conclusions from them which are of use. To be sure, if the measurements could be made, more could be concluded; but this is not the same as saying that, if the measurements cannot be made, nothing can be concluded. We therefore move on to the second part of our conditional question: why, then, make any measurements in the laboratory? The main purpose is to see if under any conditions, however limited, the postulates of the model can be confirmed and, if not, to see how they may be modified to accord better at least with those cases. It will still be an act of faith to postulate the general existence of these new constructs, but somehow one feels less cavalier if he knows that there are two or three cases where the postulates have actually been verified."[6]

They then go on to say that at present "every indication" is that their utility model, and perhaps the game model, "will have to be made more complicated if experimental data are to be handled adequately." They develop one such more complicated model, but note that "its domain of applicability is limited and it is completely unclear how it can be utilized in game theory." In short, they are committed to the development of formal models well in advance of, or inconsistent with, warranted empirical information. Their hope seems to be that the logical and mathematical rigor of the models will in one way or another illuminate human behavior, even if those models are extremely defective as models of actual behavior.

On my view, this can be dangerous and misleading; a more productive approach would be to emphasize the testing of the postulates right from the beginning. This is not to say that

---

[6]R. Duncan Luce and Howard Raiffa, *Games and Decisions*, New York, Wiley, 1957, p. 12, pp. 36-37.

eventually the models cannot be made complicated enough to describe behavior, but only that the results are not impressive to date.

More generally, clearly conflicting views are held of what constitutes scientific inquiry, and some writers would regard the "pragmatic" approach espoused in this book as grossly mistaken. For example, Patrick Suppes, who is sympathetic to construing science as "the development of theory and the confronting of theory with quantitative data," has recently emphasized the importance of formalization. He deplores the divergence between deductive method in mathematics and in physics that he believes has developed since the publication of Newton's *Principia,* and argues that much theoretical physics is elaborated "in a fashion that is very far from satisfying modern mathematical standards."

After discussing how he believes formalization can clarify basic issues in the areas of relativity, the measurement of intensive properties, and psycholinguistics, he says:

> "Extending what I have said to other areas of science, let me conclude with a transcendental argument for formalization in science. Formalization is necessary in order to achieve objective resolution of conflict. There is no other general means of resolving conceptual conflict in science. Moreover, in a wide variety of experimental situations, there is no way to resolve disputes about the interpretation of data objectively except by careful and explicit use of the set-theoretical methods of contemporary mathematical statistics. But what is necessary is necessarily desirable, and so it is with formalization in science."[7]

Rather than taking formalization as the key to resolving scientific conflict, I have stressed evidential confirmation, for it seems to me that often a choice among conflicting theories can only be made on the basis of observable evidence. Many hypotheses about the moon, for example, enjoyed strong scientific support until the first men landed there, but shortly thereafter had to be given up or modified considerably. As we shall see, the marked

---

[7]Patrick Suppes, "The Desirability of Formalization in Science," *The Journal of Philosophy,* Vol. LXV, 1968, p. 664.

differences between Suppes and myself on scientific inquiry have consequences for questions about value measurement.

C.   A LOOK AHEAD

There seems to be no avoiding a host of issues, then, when one discusses the extent to which values can be measured scientifically. There are controversies about the nature of scientific inquiry, about what measurement is, and about what values are. Frequently these broad areas of controversy are interrelated, but those who disagree fundamentally in one of those major areas will sometimes agree to a considerable extent in another area. For convenience of exposition, such large areas of controversy are discussed separately at times, but on other occasions they are linked together as circumstances warrant.

The content of this book can now be briefly described. First, some issues in the theory of measurement are considered. Then, some typical behavioral science attempts to measure values are critically discussed. These are followed by an analysis of some philosophic value theories and their implications for measurement. No unique metric for value measurement is introduced, for the view adopted here is that valuations are forms of human behavior and as such do not require any mode of measurement other than those needed for the behavior involved.

Chapter II

SOME ISSUES IN MEASUREMENT THEORY

A. PRELIMINARY COMMENTS

According to Brian Ellis, although the "nature of measurement should . . . be a central concern of the philosophy of science . . . it has attracted little attention," and there are no traditional philosophical problems of measurement for which philosophers are expected to develop answers. Ellis further maintains that philosophers holding differing general positions should have developed differing views on measurement, but instead there is a superficial climate of agreement that results from a lack of analysis of the problems involved.[1]

I agree that philosophers have not given measurement the attention it deserves and tend not to see how controversial some of the accepted doctrines are. The purpose here, however, is not to consider in detail all or most of the general questions that could be raised about measurement. Many of the available treatments of measurement theory focus exclusively or primarily on topics such as the logical characteristics of scales, the development of taxonomies of those scales, and related matters. Although such work has its importance, I shall argue that from the working scientist's point of view, nonformal questions about the cali-

---

[1]Brian Ellis, *Basic Concepts of Measurement*, Cambridge, At the University Press, 1966, Introduction, especially pp. 1-3. Although I disagree with Ellis in many important respects, some of which are discussed later, I think his recent book is unusually lucid and that his point of view is developed admirably.

bration and control of measuring devices are of equal or greater importance.[2]

In different theories of inquiry, the approaches taken toward measurement, including such topics as the importance and usefulness of distinctions between "fundamental" and "derived" measurement, may vary considerably. A recurring notion is that measurement in the physical science areas is reasonably adequate in practice and that this is made possible theoretically by the kind of scale used, but in the behavioral areas measurements are far less satisfactory in practice, are dubious in principle, and will remain so until behavioral scientists adopt the type of scale used by physical scientists. Something of the flavor of that view is illustrated by Norman Campbell's statement that "all fundamental measurements belong to physics, which might almost be described as the science of measurement."[3]

Much of the discussion of these issues was influenced by the work of a 1932 Committee, composed of physicists and psychologists, of the British Association for the Advancement of Science. In the years before that committee was appointed, considerable work had been done in the development of measures for a variety of social and psychological phenomena. The Committee's mission was to study and report on what appeared to be some of the sounder work; the possibility of "quantitative estimates of sensory events." Considerable attention was devoted to the Sone Scale of loudness, and there were disagreements as to whether or not the use of that scale resulted in the fundamental measurement of an additive property. Although there was disagreement about how the terms 'measurement' and 'quantitative estimate' are best used scientifically, many members of the Committee relied heavily on Campbell's views on measurement. The

---

[2]The philosopher who has most emphasized such issues is C. West Churchman. See, for example, the following articles by him: "A Materialist Theory of Measurement," in Roy Wood Sellars, V. J. McGill, and Marvin Farber, eds., *Philosophy for the Future*, New York, Macmillan, 1949; "Why Measure?," in C. West Churchman and Philburn Ratoosh, eds., *Measurement: Definitions and Theories*, New York, Wiley, 1959; and "On the Intercomparison of Utilities," in Sherman R. Krupp, ed., *The Structure of Economic Science*, Englewood Cliffs, Prentice-Hall, 1966.

[3]Norman R. Campbell, *Physics: The Elements*, Cambridge, At the University Press, 1920, p. 267. (Reissued as *Foundations of Science*, New York, Dover, 1957).

more conservative members of the Committee came to the conclusion that psychologists had not been able to make fundamental measurements. One question raised by Campbell and J. O. Irwin was: "Why do not psychologists accept the natural and obvious conclusion that subjective measurements of loudness in numerical terms (like those of length or weight or brightness) are mutually inconsistent and cannot be the basis of measurement?"[4]

Although the Committee's conclusions were challenged by many writers, the type of issue raised in its reports has worried many behavioral scientists working on measurement, and they often have become somewhat defensive.[5] Attention in this chapter will be focused on those general problems of measurement that have led some to believe that there are grave theoretical defects in the metrics used by behavioral scientists.

B. WHAT IS MEASUREMENT?

Most commentators agree that measurement consists in some type of application or assignment of some mathematical characteristic to something else. The "something else" is variously taken to be "reality," "things," "things and events," "conceptual entities," "properties," "quantities," "qualities," etc. The mathematical characteristic is sometimes "number," sometimes "numeral," and sometimes unspecified, and the distinctions involved may be the subject of considerable technical discussion.[6] Without in the slightest denying the importance of those issues, our main concern will be with what type of assignment of numbers to things and events constitutes scientific measurement.

---

[4]A. Ferguson, *et al.*, "Quantitative Estimates of Sensory Events," *Annual Report*, British Association for the Advancement of Science, London, 1938; A. Ferguson, *et al.*, "Quantitative Estimates of Sensory Events: Final Report," *Advancement of Science*, Vol. I, 1940, p. 338.

[5]See, for example, R. J. Bartlett, "Measurement in Psychology," *Advancement of Science*, Vol. I, 1940; and S. S. Stevens, "Measurement, Psychophysics, and Utility," in Churchman and Ratoosh, *op. cit.*, especially pp. 22 ff.

[6]For examples of various such views, see: Campbell, *op. cit.*, pp. 267-268, pp. 282-283; Karl Menger, "Mensuration and other Mathematical Connections of Observable Material," in Churchman and Ratoosh, *op. cit.*, p. 97; and Peter Caws, "Definition and Measurement in Physics," in Churchman and Ratoosh, *op. cit.*, pp. 5-6.

Many writers are anxious that 'measurement' not be given too restricted a referent. Thus S. S. Stevens says:

> "The reach of this concept [measurement] is becoming enlarged to include as measurement the assignment of numerals to objects or events according to a rule—any rule. Of course, the fact that numerals can be assigned under different rules leads to different kinds of scales and different kinds of measurement, not all of equal power and usefulness. Nevertheless, provided a consistent rule is followed, some form of measurement is achieved."[7]

Other writers argue that this type of approach is too permissive. Peter Caws, for example, says:

> *"Measurement is the assignment of particular mathematical characteristics to conceptual entities in such a way as to permit (1) an unambiguous mathematical description of every situation involving the entity and (2) the arrangement of all occurrences of it in a quasi-serial order."*

'Quasi-serial' here refers to situations in which, for any two occurrences, they are either "equivalent with respect to the property in question or that one is greater than the other."[8]

And Ellis objects strongly to the notion that "any rule" will do:

> "(a) Measurement is the assignment of numerals to things according to any determinative, non-degenerate rule.
>
> (b) We have a scale of measurement if and only if we have such a rule."

For him, a rule is determinative if "the same numerals (or ranges of numerals) would always be assigned to the same things under the same conditions," provided that "sufficient care is exercised." A nondegenerate rule allows for assigning different numerals (or ranges) to different things, or, given different conditions, to the

---

[7]Stevens, *op. cit.*, p. 19.

[8]Caws, *op. cit.*, pp. 5-6.

same thing. (An example of a degenerate rule is "Assign the number 2 to everything.")[9]

I am sympathetic to Ellis' approach here, but think much more emphasis needs to be given to the problems encountered in ascertaining when "sufficient care is exercised." Assigning the same numbers to the same things under the same conditions is often extremely difficult in practice, even if the rule used logically allows for that. As Churchman says in his criticism of Stevens:

> "Measurement is not merely the assignment of numbers to phenomena according to a rule; such a description ignores the empirical methodology completely. Measurement also includes all the operations required to calibrate and control. Measurement is essentially teleological, not merely structural. Its purpose is to provide a wide use of important information; the structure of this information is important, of course, but so are all of the control operations required to transmit the data so that it can meaningfully be applied in other places at other times. Furthermore, one cannot decide whether a given measurement process provides information of a certain structural kind without knowing the calibration and control method."[10]

At this point, I believe, we run head-on into the type of problem often encountered when the most adequate specification for a term is being discussed. Are there processes that all (or most) of us agree constitute measurement, and is our task simply that of finding the best verbal description of that process? The answer seems clearly to be "no," as is evidenced by various disputes about the type of measurement, if any, achieved by behavioral scientists. The situation is roughly as follows: There are certain processes that almost all of us would take as good examples of measuring, although there may be disagreement as to the exact nature of those processes. Then there are other processes, which some would include under the label "measurement," and others would not. In discussing measurement some terms are used more or less in their ordinary senses, while other terms are given technical uses

---

[9]Ellis, *op. cit.*, p. 41.

[10]Churchman, "On the Intercomparison of Utilities," p. 254.

within a particular context of inquiry. In short, a primary problem is the evaluation of various possible uses of the basic terms.

In recent literature, probably because of the influence of contemporary Oxford philosophy, one often finds ordinary language uses emphasized. Ellis, for example, says:

> "Sometimes it makes sense to say that two things are equal to one another in some respect when it makes no sense to say that one is greater or less than the other in this respect. For example, we can say two things are equal or the same in colour or shape, but we cannot say that one thing is greater or less than another in colour or shape. An equality of this type may be described as a *qualitative* equality. However, if two things can be said to be equal in respect to some *quantity,* it must also make sense to say that one is greater or less than the other in this respect. It is with this kind of equality, namely *quantitative* equality, that we are concerned"[11]

In my view, the hazards of relying on appeals to ordinary use in such contexts are great. For example, I would not be inclined to say under normal circumstances that two things were *equal* in shape or in color; I would only say they had the *same* color or shape. Further, I can imagine situations in which people might be willing to make comparative judgments of colors and shapes using words such as 'greater' or 'less.' In drawing freehand circles, for example, one might say that the first circle is less round than the second, and it does not sound unordinary to say that one red patch is less red than another. (I do not think Ellis intends to refer to the total amount of shape, in the sense of one object's having more shape in general than another. Even if he has that in mind, however, perhaps there are situations in which it would be said that one object has more shape than another, or that one object has more color than another.) My view is that in measurement the major terminological concern is finding uses that we can justify in the light of the problem at hand; whether or not those uses square fully with ordinary language is relatively unimportant.

---

[11]Ellis, *op. cit.,* p. 26.

To conclude this section, the general context in which we talk about measurement is important. One reason the measurement of lengths is often taken as a paradigm is that it is so useful in fostering increased prediction and control. Although obviously there are conventional elements in our measurements of length, those measurements lead to many warranted assertions about aspects and phases of the cosmos with which we are concerned; our success in prediction and control suggests that our measurements are not arbitrary. As soon as emphasis is put on prediction and control, a variety of nonformal aspects of measurement become significant. Such considerations will be taken up in Section D, but first some relevant background material will be discussed.

C. TRANSACTIONALISM

Discussions of the most fruitful way to approach the subject matter of scientific inquiry have generated an extensive literature; many of those issues were mentioned in Chapter I. The topic of concern in the present section is related to a host of issues discussed under such headings as "atomism vs. holism," "reductionism," "reality of societal laws," "methodological individualism," etc. Of immediate concern are questions relating to the unit of analysis chosen for inquiry (especially in the behavioral sciences), and on the structure and dynamics of that unit. The view taken here is closely related to the *transactionalism* of John Dewey and Arthur F. Bentley, to Norman Cameron's *biosocial* approach, and to J. R. Kantor's *interactionism*.[12] For present purposes, using the Dewey-Bentley terminology seems desirable.

Dewey and Bentley differentiate sharply between *self-action, interaction,* and *transaction.* Their preliminary account follows:

[12]John Dewey and Arthur F. Bentley, *Knowing and the Known,* Boston, Beacon Press, 1949, paperback ed., 1960. Norman Cameron, *The Psychology of Behavior Disorders: A Biosocial Interpretation,* Boston, Houghton Mifflin, 1947. J. R. Kantor, *Psychology and Logic,* Bloomington, Principia Press, Vol. I, 1945, Vol. II, 1950. Although Dewey and Bentley differentiate sharply between a transactional and an interactional approach, there is a strong family resemblance between Kantor's *interaction* and their *transaction.* The complex of issues discussed in this section is discussed in much more detail in my *Methodology of the Behavioral Sciences,* Ch. 3.

"*Self-action:* where things are viewed as acting under their own powers.

Inter-action: where thing is balanced against thing in causal interconnection.

Trans-action: where systems of description and naming are employed to deal with aspects and phases of action, without final attribution to 'elements' or other presumptively detachable or independent 'entities,' 'essences,' or 'realities,' and without isolation of presumptively detachable 'relations' from such detachable 'elements.' "[13]

They argue that a self-actional approach dominated early physics, and is illustrated by the belief that rain is caused by Jupiter Pluvius. 'Substance,' 'essence,' 'actor,' 'creator,' etc., are terms often made heavy use of in self-actional approaches. Galileo's inquiries marked the overthrow of that approach in physics. In the behavioral science areas, those who put primary emphasis on motives, intentions and purposes often use a self-actional framework. Interactionism tended to dominate in scientific inquiry until recently, and is typified by Newtonian mechanics. Many such interactional frameworks still work efficiently in that warranted assertions emerge. On the other hand, in many areas of inquiry the use of that framework produces problems that are primarily methodogenic (i.e., artifacts of the method), as is illustrated by epistemological systems which generate problems as to how mind and matter, assumed to exist in separate ontological realms, can interact.[14]

In many situations, transactionalism seems a more appropriate framework for inquiry. Take the case of a man hunting a rabbit:

"No one would be able successfully to speak of the hun*ter* and the hun*ted* as isolated with respect to hun*ting*. Yet it is just as absurd to set up hun*ting* as an event in isolation from the spatio-temporal connections of all the components."

Dewey and Bentley go on to compare a billiard game with a loan:

---

[13]Dewey and Bentley, *op. cit.*, p. 108.

[14]*Ibid.*, pp. 108-112. I have borrowed the term 'methodogenic' from Marvin Farber, *Basic Issues of Philosophy*, New York, Harper & Row, 1968, pp. 83 ff.

"If we confine ourselves to the problem of the balls on the billiard table, they can be profitably presented and studied interactionally. But a cultural account of the game in its full spread of social growth and human adaptations is already transactional. And if one player loses money to another we cannot even find words in which to organize a fully interactional account by assembling together primarily separate items. Borrower cannot borrow without lender to lend, nor lender lend without borrower to borrow, the loan being a transaction that is identifiable only in the wider transaction of the full legal-commercial system in which it is present as occurrence."[15]

In the investigation of many processes, the inquirer himself is in common process with what is being inquired into. For present purposes, then, 'transaction' designates the full ongoing process in a field in which the inquirer may be in reciprocal relation with many aspects and phases of that field. No mysticism should be attached to 'field'; it names the cluster of connected things and events found in mutual (reciprocal) relation. In many situations, a methodological emphasis on presumed self-actors, or on presumed separates interacting, does not seem as fruitful in facilitating prediction as does an emphasis on the transactional system as a whole.

The holistic emphasis on a field or system in which the aspects and phases are in common process is sometimes associated with a "tender-minded" or a "soft-science" approach as contrasted to the "tough-minded" or "hard-science" approach of more atomistic emphases. The view chosen here combines a hard-science, skeptical, tough-minded outlook with a holistic frame of reference, because such an approach seems the most fruitful for inquiry. For example, I see nothing at all mystical or tender-minded about viewing loans, borrowers, and lenders as aspects of a common transactional framework. Indeed, leaving out the "system" in which the behavior occurs is surely to make unnecessary problems and difficulties. Separating the borrower from the loaning transaction does not make inquiry more scientific; it tends to obscure some important relations.

15Dewey and Bentley, *op. cit.*, p. 133.

As applied to measurement, a transactional framework leads one to emphasize what often is ignored by philosophers: the methodological and other problems of the data-collector or person who is trying to measure something. Viewed transactionally, many aspects or phases of the whole transaction have their importance, including not only questions about the formal structure of the scale used and related problems, but the problems of calibrating the instruments used, controlling the observation of the results, etc. This issue will be discussed further in the context of fundamental vs. derived measurement; for the present I will only point out that having a scale characterized by an impressively neat and tidy set of formal properties may be of no use at all to an investigator if the conditions encountered make it impossible for him to exercise adequate control over the observations necessary for the use of that scale.

Within the framework of the last two sections, one can avoid certain troublesome problems about "genuine" vs. "artificial" quantities. Ellis is concerned about that issue, and says:

"People can be arranged in a linear order, for example, by taking the product of their height and age. Let us say that they are then arranged in order of 'hage.' But we do not think that 'hage' is the name of a genuine quantity like temperature or momentum. Hence, if the suggested formal criterion is adopted, we must be prepared to distinguish between genuine and artificial quantities. It seems better, therefore, to reject the existence of a set of linear ordering relationships as being alone a sufficient condition for the existence of a quantity, and impose certain further conditions."[16]

He also mentions the "physical or psychological importance" different linear ordering relationships may have, and talks about "interesting" quantities as contrasted to noninteresting ones. But it seems to me that the basic distinction, in this context, between genuine and artificial quantities may lead to a variety of methodogenic problems or difficulties that have little empirical significance. *Hage* is less important than *temperature* or *momentum*,

---

[16]Ellis, *op. cit.*, p. 31.

not because it lacks some genuineness in general, but because it seems to have little or no significance for the prediction and control of anything we find scientifically important. The kind of transactions we are interested in do not involve *hage* as a usefully differentiated phase or aspect, for it is not related in an "if. . . then" way to the processes we are investigating.

Although the homely examples below may seem trivial, I mention them because in some instances quantities that are as contrived or artificial as *hage* can be useful. In a postal system in which parcel post regulations establish limits in terms of the length and girth combined, and the weight, of a package, what in other contexts would seem a contrived and pointless quantity has its importance. Or a *discomfort index* arrived at by a combination of temperature and humidity readings may be useful in weather reporting. In short, linear ordering relationships do not come neatly packaged as genuine or artificial, and a heretofore uncombined set of relationships may become useful in fostering prediction and control. If so, such a set would seem genuine enough.

To summarize this section, measurement is here viewed in a full context that involves not only tentatively accepted relevant hypotheses and the formal aspects of the metric used, but also the operational problems of applying the metric in a given situation. To focus on only one aspect of the whole situation—formal properties of the scale—runs the risk that much of what is said is irrelevant or only marginally relevant to the problem at hand.

D. FUNDAMENTAL AND DERIVED MEASUREMENT

Much of the work done by those who regard fundamental measurement as of prime importance is based on, or related to, the work of N. R. Campbell, so his views will be considered here. Perhaps the severest critic of Campbell was C. W. Churchman, and his critique will therefore also be considered.

Closely related to questions about fundamental measurement, but separable from them, are controversies relating to what Churchman calls "fundamentalism" in science. A fundamentalist, in his terminology, is one who holds that "certain aspects of scientific inquiry have precedence over others" and that such "precedence relieves the scientist of the obligation to investigate them." He maintains, for example, that scientists collectively do not have to resort to primitive terms, basic axioms, etc., that must be accepted, and argues instead that scientific notions are all interrelated and that "the establishment of complete interrelation *is* the process of definition." He sees as one of the most dangerous applications of fundamentalism a view like Campbell's in measurement, for that view tends to cast doubt on the possibility of measurement in the behavioral sciences.[17]

One of Campbell's themes is the number of magnitudes or quantities that must be measured to yield a measure of some quantity in which we are interested. He points out that to measure *density* we have to measure two quantities, *mass* and *volume*. In contrast, we can measure *weight* without measuring any other magnitude or quantity. Fundamental magnitudes, then, are those the measurement of which do not involve or depend upon any other magnitude. Such fundamental magnitudes involve the simplest type of operation, which Campbell takes to be that of adding increments. So fundamental measurement involves additive scales: the magnitude X consists in "the number of standard things or 'units,' all equal in respect of the property, that have to be combined together in order to produce the thing equal to X in respect of the property." Length, area, and weight (or mass; see later discussion) are thus additive quantities, for they are all arrived at through additive operations.[18]

At this point, it is important to stress the difference between additive scales and fundamental measurement. There seems to be no reason to challenge the additive characteristics of most scales cited as additive, and I do not wish in the slightest to cast doubt

[17]Churchman, "A Materialist Theory of Measurement," pp. 477-480.

[18]The views of Campbell just referred to are found in *An Account of the Principles of Measurement and Calculation*, London, Longmans, Green, 1928, Ch. VII; Campbell's note in A. Ferguson, "Quantitative Estimates of Sensory Events: Final Report," p. 340; and *Physics: The Elements*, pp. 267-277. Campbell's technical uses of 'property,' 'quantity,' and 'magnitude' are discussed in the latter book on pp. 282-283; for present purposes we can ignore those distinctions.

on the general usefulness of such scales. But that is not equivalent to agreeing that fundamental measurements (as construed by Campbell) are possible. At times the fundamentalists write as if a scale meeting rigorous logical tests for additiveness almost certainly will be simple and easy to use in practice.

As Churchman urges vigorously and at length, the practicing scientist in his role as data-collector and evaluator is almost certain to ask questions about the measurement, say, of weight. Is the context controlled so that convection currents are absent, is the balance in good working order, etc.? But to get answers to such questions, other measurements and tests are required. Campbell was disinclined in *An Account of the Principles of Measurement and Calculation* to push such questions, and instead stressed certain operations, such as interchanging the contents of the pans to see if the balance was affected.

Campbell holds that questions about controlling the context in which the measurements are made can be "actually dangerous," since the answers involve the theory of the balance, and we then would be basing the measurements on theory, rather than the other way around. He argues that we should avoid such theoretical questions and try out the objects on the pan in order to see if the formal conditions of additivity are conformed to. He tended to answer questions about estimating the correctness of the results along the lines of his statement about ascertaining lengths: it "depends upon judgments of the contiguity of parts of lines, which is a relation instinctively perceived. . . ."[19]

Churchman is extremely critical of this approach, and asks how we know that different people instinctively perceive alike, or that a given person perceives the same way at different times. He discusses evidence indicating that:

> "Different observers *do* perceive 'instinctively' in different ways, even when the operations are very carefully specified. Further, different observers get significantly different results on different days, in different laboratories, etc."

---

[19]Campbell, *An Account of the Principles of Measurement and Calculation*, pp. 36-37, p. 271.

He goes on to note that in the so-called "exact" physical sciences such variability is often observed:

> "For example, in the case of one operation, the very 'simple' procedure of counting the grains in a certain well marked area of brass strip led to very significant differences between laboratories. Again, the simple operation of placing an explosive on a steel anvil and dropping a specified weight on it from a specified height, resulted in wide differences."[20]

In short, in actual measuring transactions, the physical scientists would seem to need a great deal of help from psychological studies of perception; what is simple, fundamental, etc., in terms of the logical structure of a metric may be highly complex from the point of view of actual measurement. In addition, and perhaps even more important, the most successful measurements may depend on a long history of scientific effort.

Churchman emphasizes that exact measurements take place in an "idealized" environment, and the results of a performed experiment are estimates of what would happen under ideal conditions. When we say that the length of a line is what would be obtained if we could put the object beside a standard meter rod, if we could exactly align the end points with standard markers, if we could control the temperature, and so on, we are talking about ideal circumstances that we cannot fully control. Our actual observations are adjusted to conform to warranted assertions arrived at (often) after a long history of scientific progress. He goes on to say:

> "But estimating what would happen in these idealized conditions requires all the science we have at our disposal; none of the so-called 'actual' operations we perform is basic, in the sense that we *infer* concerning the idealized environment from what is 'given.' The problem of what is actually given is again an idealized experiment, just as the determination of a 'direct observation' requires setting up idealized conditions."[21]

Campbell, of course, is well aware of many of the difficulties

[20]Churchman, "A Materialist Theory of Measurement," pp. 484-486.
[21]*Ibid.*, p. 489.

Churchman mentions. Indeed, in an earlier work than Churchman criticizes, Campbell mentions some of those issues indirectly. However, he tended there either to say that those problems were not aspects of measurement, but of something else, or that they concern tests of whether or not the formal conditions of measurement have been met. For example, in discussing the conditions of accurate weighing, he mentions that most of the calibration tests, etc., turn out to be examinations of whether or not what he calls the second law of addition [the magnitude of a system produced by the addition of bodies A, B, C, . . . depends only on the magnitude of those bodies and not on the order or method of their addition] is fulfilled. Warnings to insure that the bodies being weighed are at the same temperature as the balance are "directed against conditions in which that law is known to be false."[22]

Some of the differences between the approaches of Churchman and Campbell come out clearly in the latter's discussion of why he takes *mass* as fundamental even though what actually is measured is *weight*:

> "What is actually measured in the fundamental process of weighing is the weight of a body in air at a given region of the earth's surface relative to the weight in the same air at the same place of the standard unit body. If all bodies are of equal density, we believe that their weights measured in this way are proportional to their masses; if they are not, a 'correction' involving the densities of the bodies and of air, is introduced, and it is believed that the values so corrected are proportional to the mass. But this belief depends upon the truth of some proposition *which is not involved in weighing at all;* what is its nature, whether it is a numerical law, a definition or a theory, is a question of some difficulty. . . . However, owing to the necessity for the correction, mass, so defined, is measured by a process which is not truly fundamental. But for our present purpose it will be convenient and permissible to overlook this fact. . . . The inaccuracy would raise difficulties only if we inquired into the reason why force and energy are given dimensions in terms of mass, length and time; . . . these difficulties. . . belong properly to a much later stage of our inquiry. . . ."

22Campbell, *Physics: The Elements,* pp. 284-285.

And Campbell also says that the "possibility of measurement at every stage depends entirely upon the assumption of certain experimental laws."[23]

Such remarks seem to bear out Churchman's contentions. The distinction and relation between *mass* and *weight*, for example, depend on much scientific inquiry, and surely the "corrections" mentioned by Campbell may be vital for accurate measurement. And if it is permissible to overlook the "nonfundamental" characteristic of *mass*, surely the nonfundamentalness of some other quantities, such as those measured by behavioral scientists, can similarly be overlooked. To say arbitrarily that what is necessary to correct an actually observed weight "is not involved in weighing at all" is peculiar and misleading. In short, since Campbell here seems to agree with Churchman about the many things that must be done to insure reliable measurement, why insist that they are not "involved" in weighing?

In my opinion, these difficulties are not overcome by Campbell's revised views in his later book, where he maintains that what is measured on a balance is *mass*, not *weight*. He says:

> "Weight is a property determined both by the body and the gravitational field in which it is placed; mass is a property determined only by the body and independent of the gravitational field. In using a balance we employ the property weight. . . . But the property actually determined is mass, not weight; the equality of bodies determined by the balance is independent of the gravitational field, so long as it is uniform. That seems to me a perfectly valid reason why *weight* is not a suitable name for the property determined by the balance. But there is a further complication which makes it doubtful whether *mass* is the appropriate term; it is that the property determined by the balance, though independent of the gravitational field, is dependent on the density of air. . . . The truth is that, if we are to take this complication into account, we want a third term, balance-mass, in addition to dynamical mass and weight; but if we have to use existing terms, *mass* is better than *weight*."[24]

---

[23]*Ibid.*, pp. 378-379, p. 286. (My italics.)
[24]Campbell, *An Account of the Principles of Measurement and Calculation,* p. 45.

The issues raised by Campbell's remarks illustrate the importance in measurement both of "theory" and of our choice of terminology. The apparent straightforward simplicity of fundamental measurement turns out to be quite complicated in practice.

None of the foregoing is to say that in measurement the problems just described are always acute, not is it to suggest that Campbell's position could not be refined and improved. Quite often even contemporary accounts, however, rely on something close to Campbell's approach; as Ellis points out, much of Campbell's work has been basically accepted. One recurring theme is that some measurements do not depend on "anything else," and hence have great importance in science.

For example, in an influential article Bergmann and Spence argued that statements about certain physical relations (*greater than, equal to*) "can be tested by the scientist's observations or *manipulations within the dimension.*" They go on:

> "Manipulations within a dimension do not involve utilization of any of the empirical laws which connect it with other dimensions. The manipulations, for instance, by which we compare the lengths of yardsticks and build their operational sum. . . lie entirely within the dimension of length. That is to say, the empirical laws which make length an extensive dimension are the axioms of extensity. . . . And these laws have no reference to any other dimension."[25]

But as we shall see in Section F, establishing standards for length is very complicated and seems to depend on the full development of science, including the manipulation of many dimensions.

To take another example, although Ellis notes that "even for fundamental measurement" we need "criteria for equality," he goes on to say:

> "All measurement ultimately depends on certain basic forms of measurement. If, for example, we can measure length, then

---

25Gustav Bergmann and Kenneth W. Spence, "The Logic of Psychophysical Measurement," *Psychological Review*, Vol. 51, 1944. Reprinted as "Psychophysical Measurement," in Melvin H. Marx, ed., *Psychological Theory*, New York, Macmillan, 1951. The quotations are from Marx, p. 261, p. 263.

we can measure volume; and if we can measure volume, we can measure temperature. But length measurement need not depend on anything else. Like mass, time-interval, electrical resistance and potential difference, length may be measured directly."[26]

It is interesting to note that Ellis here, like others, uses the phrase 'need not depend on anything else,' when what is apparently intended is 'need not depend on the measurement of any other *type* of quantity,' or perhaps, 'does not formally depend on anything else.' Any actual measurement may depend on a whole host of other factors, and the fact that no other type of quantity is involved may not be much of an advantage. In carrying out measurements, the control of what needs to be controlled can be among the most difficult of the tasks involved. In some instances, measurements depending on the measurement of other magnitudes may be more reliable, useful, and successful than direct, "fundamental" measurements. Talking about the independence of measurement from "anything else" is likely to suggest some basic or elementary starting point that is effectively beyond criticism.

We have, then, two contrasting strategies of research. In one, some unchallengeable, sound, fundamental, or basic starting point is searched for; once that is achieved, other work is erected on that base. The other strategy assumes that *all* aspects of scientific inquiry are open to criticism and improvement, and views scientific progress in terms of achieving more adequately described and articulated relations, rather than in terms of an architectonic layering. The question becomes one of which strategy is most productive in the context of measurement. The fundamentalist's emphasis on the distinction between the formal requirements of a scale and whether or not given measurement operations conform to those requirements often turns out to be deceptive; ascertaining whether or not given measurement processes conform to the formal properties regarded as desirable in a scale involves us in just the difficulties the fundamentalist hoped to avoid. The theoretical and empirical simply cannot be separated in such inquiries without distortion.

26Ellis, *op. cit.*, p. 2, p. 53, p. 74.

To illustrate, we noted earlier in some detail the difficulties Campbell had about the fundamentalness of *mass*. Mass is something that, given the history of physics, should be a fundamental magnitude if a view like Campbell's is to be plausible, and yet inquiry into the measurements of mass suggest that it is nonfundamental. (This is not to say that mass necessarily is a nonfundamental magnitude, but only to point out that a rather elaborate rationalization is necessary to make it so.) Even in less complicated cases, the same interrelation between the formal and the empirical seems to occur.

For example, let us look at Campbell's criticism of the Mohs Scale of hardness in mineralogy. The hardness of a mineral is determined by its ability to scratch, or to be scratched by, one of the standard minerals that are arranged in an order of increasing hardness (from talc to diamond). Campbell is critical of that scale because the formal conditions he thinks are necessary for something to be a measurable property are not achieved. Specifically, two minerals, neither of which can scratch the other, may yet have different potentialities for scratching a third mineral. (Technically, taking the relation we are concerned with as *scratches,* in the Mohs Scale that relation is not always a transitive asymmetrical one.)[27] But how do we know that the Mohs Scale fails to meet the criteria Campbell sets up? To test that, we are involved in the type of empirical problem Churchman emphasizes. Such problems in the case of the Mohs Scale are not difficult or troublesome, but we still have to take pains to see that various relevant aspects of the situation are controlled.

Would it not be sensible, then, to view the Mohs Scale in a developmental perspective? We probably would conclude that for some purposes, at a given stage in the development of mineralogy such a scale was useful and led to predictions that otherwise could not have been made. The defects and deficiencies of the Mohs scale would not thereby be overlooked, but might well serve as a stimulus to either improving it or to developing a better scale. The fundamentalists tend to urge tests for measurement that on the one hand can lead to a rejection of useful scales,

---

[27]Campbell, *An Account of the Principles of Measurement and Calculation,* p. 7.

and on the other hand can lead to the glossing over of calibration and control problems.

E. PRESENT VIEW OF MEASUREMENT

The view of measurement tentatively taken in this volume combines some of the views of Ellis and of Churchman. Rather than taking measurement as the assignment of numbers according to any rule, the restriction proposed by Ellis seems to have great merit; we need what he calls a "determinative, non-degenerate rule" and we "have a scale if and only if we have such a rule." But from the point of view of measurement as a transaction, other considerations of the type urged by Churchman can be of equal or greater importance.

In general, the purpose of measurement is to provide a certain class of important warranted information applicable to a wide variety of problems and situations. The logical structure or ordering of that information is important, but so also are the operations through which the information is gained and transmitted. As Churchman says: "Control in measurement is for the sake of treating an object in the most effective manner relative to any problem." He goes on to say that if we know the "exact" length of an object, then in any situation in which length is a critical property, we have important information. But having the "exact" length alone is not enough for the efficient scientific use of the object. We also need information about the other relevant properties of the object and its context, as well as information about the warranted assertions covering changes in those properties. Adequate scaling for the property in question does provide the information needed with respect to *that* property.[28]

Moreover, the general effectiveness of measurement, scaling, etc., must be judged in terms of all the relevant scientific information at our command. As noted, there may be important problems about the perception of aligning markers, etc. For

---

[28]Churchman, "A Materialist Theory of Measurement," pp. 490-491; "Why Measure?," p. 84; "On the Intercomparison of Utilities," p. 254.

present purposes, even more important is the funded scientific information available. Churchman mentions a typical situation involving data from several scientific disciplines:

> "An experimenter wishes to see if there is any correlation between two variables, let us say the amount of soot fall and the incidence of tuberculosis, or the amount of steel produced and the salary rate of steel workers, or blood pressure and temperament. The too common procedure is to set up 'scales,' in the formal sense, for measuring the variables, to accumulate a good many paired observations, and then to run a correlation analysis. And the results often mean nothing in the pragmatic sense. Suppose the amount of soot fall *is* correlated with the incidence of tuberculosis. What then? What should we do? Is this a sufficient basis for clearing areas of smoky conditions in order to reduce tuberculosis? Not at all. The soot may fall heavily in areas where people are economically poor, and hence poorly nourished. Thus, the soot fall could be reduced, and the incidence of tuberculosis remain unchanged."[29]

He goes on to add that of course we could "fix up" the tuberculosis experiment, but the point is how to avoid making the same kind of mistake on yet another level. The scientifically efficient use of an object, and its measurement, require a grasp of the relation of the property measured to its other properties and to the properties of other objects in the situation under investigation.

As judged in terms of the development of scientific inquiry, then, technical problems of the measurement of some phenomenon may be of lesser significance than how we view the phenomenon being measured. Especially in behavioral science fields there may be great disagreement about the referents of the key terms involved. To illustrate, Martin Bronfenbrenner has scathingly criticized one index of inflation on the ground that the index is founded as much on the "quality" of money (judged in terms of its backing) as on the quantity of money or the observed changes in prices, and goes so far as to suggest that it is "doubtful" that

---

[29]Churchman, "A Materialist Theory of Measurement," pp. 492-493.

"complete academic freedom" should be granted for such views.[30] The index in question is based on the view that inflating is "the creation of purchasing media in excess of the amount needed for representing things being processed and offered in the markets." 'Purchasing media' is used to refer both to currency and to demand deposits.[31]

Without entering into the merits of the contrasting economic views on this issue, several aspects of the controversy can be noted. Differing views about the referent for 'money' and 'inflation' are involved, as well as differing views as to the most appropriate methodology for inquiry into economics. What is an excellent index of inflation in one sense of 'inflation' may be a poor index in another sense of that term. As is so often the case in behavioral inquiry, we are faced with many serious decisions as to how to proceed, and we must deal with questions as to which approach will be most useful in the prediction and control of economic phenomena. To assume that we have only a technical problem about measurement would be blind.

Suppose, for the sake of argument, that we have narrowed the field to two possible indices of inflation. And let us further assume that the two referents of 'inflation' involved are clearly stated. We then have two classes of problems, although they are interrelated. We can ask how effectively the first index represents what it is supposed to represent, and the same for the second index. But no matter how technically impressive one of those indices is, it may be of little or no use if the notion of inflation it is based on is scientifically unsound. And the other index, even if it is not as adequate as one that later may be developed, can still be useful if it helps to describe states of affairs that are significantly linked to economic behavior.

Lest some of the foregoing be misunderstood, let me emphasize certain points. In investigating inflation, I am not at all saying that we should take any particular use of 'inflation' for

---

30Martin Bronfenbrenner, "A 'Middlebrow' Introduction to Economic Methodology," in Krupp, *op. cit.*, p. 22, p. 24.

31*Research Reports*, Great Barrington, American Institute for Economic Research, June 10, 1968, p. 95.

granted, even if it has the support of many economists. Extensive inquiries into the evidence are necessary before a use is tentatively taken as the most suitable, and what at first sight may seem to be a questionable use may turn out to be the scientifically most productive one. Once a tentative use is selected, then technical questions about the index or other measures are appropriate, and that in turn may pose many difficult problems. We need to be skeptically critical at all stages of the inquiry. Unlike some commentators, I see no *basic* theoretical difference here between the physical and the behavioral areas; the difference seems to be that physical scientists have reached agreement, based on scientific evidence, about the specifications of their key terms more often than have behavioral scientists. To return to the area of value measurement, I think the problems associated with the specification of key terms presently have greater importance than problems about the scales used.

F.   CONCLUDING COMMENTS

From the point of view taken here, measurement is construed in its full transactional context. Its importance in scientific inquiry stems from the facilitation of predictions; i.e., successful quantification allows more accurate predictions than otherwise would be possible. Just what level of precision is necessary and useful depends upon the context and our purposes, and the relative success of the techniques employed also depends on those purposes. Again from the vantage point of performing measuring operations, the reliability and adequacy of measurement for the purposes at hand are of the utmost importance. The effectiveness of any measure involves much more than the formal properties of the scale used.

Further, in practice, technological problems are likely to be intermeshed with theoretical problems. As Allen Astin argues, the task of finding more accurate ways of measuring physical phenomena never ends. To provide mensurational units that can be reproduced with high fidelity, emphasis is placed on linking those units to "basic constants of nature," preferably at the atomic

level. Length, time, and temperature have been specified in terms
of such basic constants, but mass has not as yet.

Even when that is achieved (as in the revised standard for
length), further improvement may be possible. Astin describes
the new standard as follows:

> "In October, 1960, the 11th General Conference of Weights
> and Measures redefined the meter as 1,650,763.73 wavelengths in
> a vacuum of the reddish-orange radiation emitted by the transi-
> tion between energy levels $2p_{10}$ and $5d_5$ of the krypton-86 atom.
> The radiation is emitted when atoms excited to the $5d_5$ level fall
> to the $2p_{10}$ level. The accuracy of the old standard, in effect
> since 1889, was limited by the accuracy with which two meter
> bars could be compared: about one or two parts in 10 million.
> The krypton-86 standard improves on this accuracy by a factor
> of 10."

But the new standard also has its difficulties. Astin says the
main defect is that in a single step it cannot measure distances as
long as one meter. He suggests that perhaps a laser wavelength
standard may make possible measuring path differences of tens or
hundreds of meters in one step, but that it will be necessary to
demonstrate that "laser wavelengths are sufficiently stable and
reproducible" before such an international standard can be
accepted.[32]

Despite all that has been said above, the advantages of additive scales in a wide range of contexts is impressive, and much
effort to develop additive scales in situations where they do not
yet exist probably would be justified. I have much greater reser-
vations about emphasizing the merits of fundamental measurements, understood as measurements only of one quantity or
magnitude.

The more magnitudes involved in a given measurement,
other things being equal, the greater the possibility of error, but
such errors need to be viewed in comparison with other errors,
indeterminacies, and difficulties. Quite likely situations occur in

---

[32]Allen V. Astin, "Standards of Measurement," *Scientific American*, Vol. 218, No. 6,
June, 1968, p. 50, p. 57.

which the latter type of error is far greater than errors stemming from the measurement of more than one magnitude. Some measurements of length (a supposed direct and fundamental measurement) may be far more inaccurate under the best laboratory circumstances now available than some measurements of temperature relying on the measurement of volume (and hence indirect and nonfundamental) under the best available conditions. And as we have just seen, the standard of length now accepted has associated with it a host of technological issues; the "directness" of measurements of length can be misleading.

In general, then, much depends on whether scientific inquiry is viewed as a human effort designed to facilitate prediction and control, or whether it is judged in terms of the formal perfection of the "logic" of inquiry. The first approach is adopted throughout this book.

Chapter III

SUBJECTIVE VS. OBJECTIVE BASES
FOR VALUE MEASUREMENT

A. PURPOSE OF CHAPTER

This chapter is concerned with the contrasting views of two psychologists, L. L. Thurstone and Clark L. Hull. A consideration of their views will help to illustrate much that was said earlier and to provide a useful basis for later chapters. Thurstone maintained that human values are "essentially subjective" and that a subjective metric must be established to measure them, while Hull argued that the processes involved in value and valuation can be treated objectively "by the quantitative methodology of natural science."[1] Thurstone and Hull were chosen for discussion because their views illustrate two major possible approaches in value measurement.

Both Thurstone and Hull agree that values can be satisfactorily measured, and both look forward to seeing many areas of inquiry that presently are not pursued scientifically becoming scientific. Their views on the subjective-objective issue, however, are in basic opposition. Many related matters are involved, including questions about the most useful referents for the basic terms used in the controversy. As argued earlier, then, controversies about the possibility of measuring values become en-

---

[1] L. L. Thurstone, "The Measurement of Values," *Psychological Review*, Vol. 61, 1954, p. 47. Clark L. Hull, "Value, Valuation, and Natural-Science Methodology," *Philosophy of Science*, Vol. 11, 1944, p. 130.

meshed in a variety of other issues, including questions about the nature of scientific inquiry and the nature of value.

For present purposes, I want to emphasize the terminological problems encountered in the use of 'value.' Discussions about the measurement of value sometimes lack any reasonably clear and specific account of the author's use of 'value,' and where such a use is specified it often is not the one urged by other workers. Unfortunately, such matters are often de-emphasized or overlooked by behavioral scientists. In recent years, many analytic philosophers have assumed that although value terms are used in diverse ways in ordinary discourse, those uses are in general appropriate, correct, and sensibly interconnected. In contrast, the philosophical naturalists in value theory often argued that because of the diversity, vagueness, etc., found in ordinary discourse about values, the task is to select or develop some use that could be taken as central and which would lead to some changes or reform in ordinary language.[2]

The latter approach was out of favor for some time, and so it is interesting to note a recent statement by the analytic philosopher, Richard Brandt:

> ". . . value-words, in their ordinary use, are very vague, and the authors of value-statements do not have any definite meaning in mind when they make them. Moreover, there is some reason to think that what meaning they have varies a good deal from one person to another, the extent depending largely upon the cultural history of the individual. What is called for, in contrast to laboring with ordinary usage, is that we *assign* some definite meaning to these terms, doubtless within the rough and vague limits prescribed by present usage, and that we do so for definite, statable, and relevant reasons."[3]

This is very much in line with how such naturalists as Ralph B. Perry and Stephen C. Pepper construed their task, so perhaps their views will again be taken seriously. In any event, it is

---

[2]These issues are discussed at considerable length in Rollo Handy, *Value Theory and the Behavioral Sciences*, Springfield, Charles C Thomas, 1969, Chs. I, II, and III.

[3]Richard B. Brandt, "The Concept of Welfare," in Sherman R. Krupp, ed., *The Structure of Economic Science*, Englewood Cliffs, Prentice-Hall, 1966, p. 261.

assumed here that although the use selected for 'value' should be
such that the field to which the term refers will overlap considerably the field referred to in ordinary language, the results of
scientific inquiry into human valuating behavior should be the
main determinant of the specification of 'value.'[4]

B.   THURSTONE'S VIEWS

Thurstone does not offer a formal or official statement as
to his use of 'value', although from the examples he cites it
seems clear that at least much of the time he takes *choice* or
preference as central in valuations. He emphasizes that sometimes quite subtle distinctions may be involved. For example,
in discussing the measurement of social attitudes he mentions a
study of attitudes toward Prohibition that was based on questionnaire responses. What the subjects said on the attitude scale
was then compared to the subjects' "actual" or "overt" behavior,
and it was found that there was considerable agreement.
Thurstone goes on to say that although such a comparison is
interesting, it is not "a validation of the attitude scale." A person may show complete consistency between what he says and
what he does about some issue, but his actual attitude (in the
sense of "affective disposition") may be quite different. A good
friend in private and in confidence may be able to elicit what
the subject genuinely feels about the matter, even though those
feelings will not be expressed in public. Thurstone concludes
that "attitudes are essentially subjective experiences which may
or may not conform with overt action."[5]

Because of his emphasis on the subjectivity of values,
Thurstone sees as a basic problem the establishment of a "subjective metric." Such a metric is to be used wherever the phenomena to be measured cannot be represented adequately by
physical objects, or where their intensities or magnitudes cannot
be physically measured. He says:

[4]See Ralph B. Perry, *Realms of Value,* Cambridge, Harvard University Press, 1954,
p. 2; Stephen C. Pepper, *The Sources of Value,* Berkeley, University of California
Press, 1958, p. 9.

[5]Thurstone, *op. cit.,* pp. 51-52.

"One of the main requirements of a truly subjective metric
is that it shall be entirely independent of all physical measurement. In freeing ourselves completely from physical measurement, we are also free to experiment with esthetic objects and
with many other types of stimuli to which there does not correspond any known physical measurement."[6]

Most of Thurstone's article is given over to two main
themes—problems relating to the establishment of a subjective
metric in general, and illustrations of value measurements using
such a metric. Considering the illustrations first will be best
for present purposes. Of the various investigations mentioned,
some deal with what Thurstone regards as trivial values and
others with socially important values, but he argues that the
basic methodological problems are the same.

One of the inquiries discussed was a study of social attitudes
toward differing nationalities. Each of the five groups of subjects
was given the same list of paired nationalities, but was asked
different questions, reflecting varying degrees of intimacy, about
those pairs. For example, in one group the question was which
of the pair you would rather associate with; in another group,
which you would rather have as a fellow student; in yet another
group, which would you rather have your sister marry; etc. The
rank-ordering of the nationalities was "essentially the same" in
all five groups, but depending on the intimacy of the context
specified, a particular nationality was favored to different degrees.

Another survey cited of "moral values" involved the presentation of paired offenses; for each pair the respondents indicated which they considered the most serious. A group of
high school students was given the test, and a short time later
was shown a film describing the life of a gambler. A few
days later they were given the test again, and finally were given
it a third time about six months later. The subjects considered
gambling to be a considerably more serious offense after seeing
the movie than they did before, and apparently retained this
attitude for some time. Thurstone goes on to say that the subjects
just described lived in small Illinois towns; when Chicago chil-

------

[6]*Ibid.,* p. 47.

dren were similarly tested, the effect of the movie was quite slight. One hypothesis was that large city residents saw so many movies that one show more or less made relatively little difference in their attitudes.

Another type of problem was illustrated from the field of market research, in which the main focus was on the "values" of a firm, but in which the "values" of its customers were also involved. If a store carrying a limited number of neckties desires to please the majority of its customers, one approach would be to determine the 20 or 30 most popular designs, and then stock those. But Thurstone argues that this would give the wrong answer, for some people would find the stock thus selected to contain many equally acceptable patterns, while other customers would find nothing to their taste. So he suggests instead that first the single most popular design be found, and then in the total sample population of customers all those who chose that pattern would be eliminated. For the remaining population, the pattern most approved would be found, and the part of the population choosing that pattern would be eliminated. This process would be continued until stocking an additional pattern would result in only a very few people preferring it. Thurstone goes on to suggest that similar procedures might be very useful under emergency conditions (such as wartime) when only a limited number of consumer goods can be produced.

A fourth project concerned the prediction of choices with respect to menus. Each subject was asked to indicate, for a list of 40 foods on an interval schedule, how much he liked or disliked each food. In addition, the subjects were presented with 16 menus and were asked what they would probably choose from each menu. The two approaches produced very similar results.

It should be noted that Thurstone's claims for the type of work cited above are modest. He describes it as "admittedly crude and exploratory," but also finds the results promising enough so that much more work should be done. In addition to the type of survey mentioned, Thurstone also discusses investigations of propaganda, group morale, voting behavior, economic utilities, and esthetic values. His attempt to develop a measure of "subjective" value, then, takes as basic those situations in which the subjects indicate a choice, or selection, or preference from among some alternatives made available to them. We will return to this point later.

Moving now to Thurstone's discussion of the development of "subjective units" for a "subjective metric," he says that satisfactory results have been achieved in studies of "comparative judgment and its variants." He illustrates his approach by an account of the problems encountered in inquiry into judgments of the excellence of handwriting. In a rough sorting of a variety of specimens of handwriting, quite good agreement is likely to be reached about those that are best and those that are poorest. But, he says, such excellence does not correspond to any physical measurement that might be made of the script. In order to circumvent problems stemming from variations in the uses of superlatives, etc., the subjects were given pairs of handwriting samples, and asked merely to say which was the better of the pair, without stating the degree of excellence. Thurstone holds that people experience the excellence of a specimen "in terms of some subjective process or quale." Better specimens are associated with some quale that differentiates them from inferior specimens. He also postulates the existence of "discriminal processes which differ in some manner in terms of which the percipient does make the discrimination." Such discriminal processes are not necessarily subjective; they "may be assumed to be physical or truly subjective according to the preferences of the investigator."

The discriminal processes that (through postulation) correspond to different values are arranged in a spectrum from best to worst. But dispersion is almost certain to be involved; when the same specimen is compared on many different occasions by a given subject, "it is not to be expected that he would always experience a particular specimen with the same discriminal process." Thurstone assumes that the spectrum of responses can be adjusted so that the frequency distribution of the discriminal processes to the same stimulus specimen is Gaussian. We thus have a metric, but so far it is arbitrary. When the same procedure is repeated for all the specimens, in many experiments the "metrics determined for the separate stimuli will be the same when all of the stimuli are considered together."

In the model being constructed, the proportion of times in which a subject judges specimen j to be better than k can be observed. Each stimulus specimen is taken as a Gaussian distribution with a mean and a discriminal dispersion; an ambiguous stimulus will be characterized by a wide dispersion. Thurstone says:

> "Each stimulus will then be defined in the subjective continuum by its mean position which is called a scale value and by the standard deviation of its dispersion of discriminal processes. Each stimulus is then defined by two parameters in the subjective continuum."[7]

In order to put numbers into these parameters, an "arbitrary origin" is chosen: the "mean value that one of the stimuli projects on the continuum." The unit of measurement is chosen arbitrarily as the standard deviation of the dispersion for that stimulus. Then similar numerical values can be given to all of the specimens, and a subjective metric has been achieved. Thurstone argues that in thus dealing with subjective quales no physical magnitudes of any kind have been assumed, but "only that in principle" the relative frequency of association of the subjective quales with any given stimulus can be ascertained. When this cannot be done directly, the frequencies can be obtained through inferences from the observed comparative data. In short, Thurstone believes that his procedure offers a way of studying stimuli "which have no physical measure whatever."

C.　CRITICISM OF THURSTONE

The type of work cited by Thurstone, as well as more recent work, is disparaged by certain critics as being trivial and of too local or parochial a nature. Those who are suspicious of any scientific study of values are likely to be quite contemptuous

---

[7]*Ibid.*, p. 49.

when they see an inquiry into menu choices cited as a scientific investigation of values. As noted, Thurstone himself emphasizes that some of the inquiries he discusses are trivial, for his concern was with the basic methodology rather than the specific content of the inquiries. And as argued earlier, merely because the generalizations arrived at do not apply to vast numbers of humans over a long time period does not necessarily mean the generalizations are either unscientific or unimportant; if our aim is the study of a small group, we need not worry if the generalizations found do not apply to other groups. In any event, the study of trivial phenomena may be useful in the study of significant phenomena; the criticisms of Thurstone made in this section will concern methodological issues.

Since the publication of Thurstone's article there has been considerable additional work done along the similar lines. The increasing sophistication of questionnaires and the development of more refined statistical techniques for handling the data should neither be overlooked nor their significance minimized. In many important respects, however, both Thurstone's work and more technically elaborate work raise the same methodological problems. Perhaps the key issue concerns just what is being inquired into by studies of the sort Thurstone emphasizes.

Historically, many philosophers have maintained that "mental" events cannot be quantitatively measured,[8] and in the previous chapter we saw the views of some physicists on that issue. In a sense Thurstone has joined such critics of psychology, for he hoped to find a subjective metric that was "entirely independent of all physical measurement" and maintained that the subjective quales dealt with do not have physical magnitudes. All this is reminiscent of some traditional mind-matter dualisms in which matter is extended (and thus measurable) while mind is not.

Thurstone constantly contrasts the "subjective" to something else, such as "overt behavior." Yet he not only fails to tell us clearly how the two are differentiated, in his examples of "sub-

---

[8]For some interesting examples, see Charles E. Spearman, *Psychology Down the Ages*, Vol. I, London, Macmillan, 1937, pp. 89-91.

jective" measurement what he actually investigates is "overt"
behavior. In general subjective-objective dichotomies that locate
some behavior entirely within the organism generate a great
many methodological problems.[9] But even setting aside such
difficulties, and also for the moment assuming that there are
subjective quales in Thurstone's sense, it seems quite clear that
the kind of work he mentions does not somehow measure those
quales, but rather measures overt behavior that supposedly is
correlated with the subjective quales.

For example, in judging the excellence of handwriting, the
experimenter does not somehow get within the subject's "mind,"
or mental processes, or grasp hold of the subjective quales, but
rather he does something with the subject's overt responses. The
subject says which of two items he finds best, and that response
is clearly in the publicly observable world. Thurstone is faced
with the classic problems of mind-body dualisms when he attempts to account for the interaction between the two realms.
We have subjective quales, on the one hand, and overt behavior
on the other, with a "discriminal process" in between. As mentioned, Thurstone tolerantly leaves open the question of whether
the discriminal processes are "truly subjective" or are physical.
But either way, the general problem remains: how to get to the
"truly subjective" via observable behavior, and vice-versa. The
question is not so much just where the gap between the two
realms is postulated, but how to bridge that gap once it is
postulated.

Thurstone assumes, then, a kind of dualism in which
"mental events" occur and are correlated somehow with "external" events. In my opinion, a much better way of getting at
some of the distinctions he wants to make, and which are involved in the kinds of situation he wants to explore, is to talk
about various contexts of behavior.

To illustrate, let us look at a different example. Suppose
that a person is asked to estimate the length of a line without
the aid of any instruments, and that his estimate is then com-

_____

[9]A little noted but impressive paper by Arthur F. Bentley shows some of the major
problems with such dichotomies: "The Human Skin: Philosophy's Last Line of
Defense," *Philosophy of Science,* Vol. 8, 1941.

pared to the result of a careful measurement of that line. In many ways the estimates made would be similar to the type of response Thurstone talks about, but there seems little to be gained by postulating a subjective quale. Rather, we can talk about, investigate, and probably make predictions about those estimates without leaving the realm of observable behavior. We also can study other behavioral settings in which careful measurements of the line's length are made. Two types of behavioral setting are involved, and it may be interesting to compare the results obtained, but we need not say one investigation concerns the "subjective" realm and the other "overt" behavior. Indeed, some of the so-called "subjective" elements will be involved in the behavior of reading the length of the line against a standard measuring object.

Thurstone's comments about physical magnitudes also seem to exhibit terminological confusion. Clearly enough, we should not assume that the subjects judge handwriting excellence in terms of any one simple physical measurement such as, say, the height of the taller letters. But that alone does not rule out the possibility that more complex physical measurements will provide some useful predictors. If the patterns are measured, including the relative sizes and relations of the letters, etc., we *may* have something that relates to judgments of excellence. Since the subjects neither were given any specific criteria of excellence nor were asked what their own criteria were, I of course do not maintain that any of the subjects did judge handwriting excellence in terms of patterns and relationships that Thurstone would regard as physically measurable. But his implied sharp separation between what is subjective and what is physically measurable is not supported.

In my opinion, some of the more subtle points raised by Thurstone are obscured by his general methodological assumptions. Let us look at the type of example he emphasizes—the relation between a person's attitudes and his overt behavior. Suppose we have a personnel director who, on some attitude test, turns out to be free of anti-Semitism (assuming some agreed upon referent for that term). Suppose further that as a check on the validity of the test, we observe his actions as a personnel director, and find he does not discriminate against Jews in his hiring. As Thurstone emphasizes, although the correlation between the test results and his behavior on the job is interesting, we do not know that privately the person is free of anti-Semitism. Perhaps a close friend can ascertain that the person has anti-Semitic attitudes yet finds it advisable to hide those attitudes in more public settings. Thurstone says:

> "A man may be entirely consistent in what he says and in what he does about a controversial issue, and yet both of these indices may be dead wrong in reflecting his attitude. . . . His personal attitudes may or may not agree with what he says and what he does. Here again, attitudes are essentially subjective experiences which may or may not conform with overt action."[10]

In my view, Thurstone's approach is somewhat incoherent. Even the trusted friend may not get at some of the subject's attitudes; we are not necessarily any closer to the "subjective experience" than we were in observing other aspects of the person's behavior. Also, in some situations the "hidden" attitudes may be unimportant, if the person does not act in accord with them. Rather than attempting to find a person's "true" value or attitude, I suggest that a clearer approach would be to emphasize the subject's behavior in different contexts. If we know what behavior we want to predict in a particular setting, we need not, for *that* purpose, worry about other settings. The generalizations will be of the form "If a, b, c . . . , then x." When the if-clause situation changes, we expect the then-clause situation to change also.

Some critics regard the attempt to specify 'value' in terms of attitudes, interests, preferences, etc., as making values too unsettled, flexible, or unstable. They assume that values are more permanent than interests, without making values absolute or unchangeable, and therefore use 'value' as the name for something believed to be more basic in behavior. One such attempt is discussed in the next section.

---

[10]Thurstone, *op. cit.*, pp. 51-52.

As a final comment, my criticisms of Thurstone should not be understood as saying that the study of attitudes, interests, choices, preferences, etc., is either scientifically impossible or unproductive. My view is that such behavior can be measured and that accurate prediction is possible in principle. Although I think Thurstone misdescribes what he actually was doing, his account of the development of what he calls a subjective metric shows one way of assigning numbers to things that may turn out to be quite useful in predicting certain types of behavior.

D. HULL'S VIEWS

Hull begins by noting the great variation in the literature of how values and valuations are characterized, and therefore gives considerable attention to the uses for value terms that seem most promising to him. Since he is interested in a "natural science" approach to value phenomena, he also indicates in outline what he understands that approach to be. Hull's attempt to achieve clarity is helpful; his account of his views on value theory is well enough done so that those who disagree with him can easily ascertain just where they disagree and why.

In general, Hull is concerned to show that we need not adopt an introspective (or subjective) approach to the problems of value, and he argues that in principle valuative behavior can "ultimately be predicted from a knowledge of the antecedent states of the organism and the relevant environing circumstances."[11] As we shall see, although his account of scientific method is far more formalistic and positivistic than John Dewey's, Hull regards his "general approach" to the problems of value and valuation as "substantially" the same as Dewey's.

As part of what Hull calls "the elementary characteristics" of the theoretical side of natural science methodology, he holds that a "satisfactory" theory must have "a set of known postulates or primary principles." The main body of a theory consists in "theorems or secondary principles derived from" the primary principles. So that the principles can be used in deriving "quan-

---

[11]Hull, *op. cit.*, p. 126.

titative theorems which shall be unambiguously applicable to
the observable world," the terms (or signs) by means of which
the principles are stated must have referents that "are clearly
known, or at least definitely knowable." Finally, there must be
qualitative and quantitative conformity between the theorems
and the observable facts to which they refer.

Hull puts this in another way by emphasizing that a satisfactory scientific theory consists of a set of undefined signs; a
set of terms unambiguously defined on the basis of the undefined
signs; a set of primary principles or postulates that are stated
entirely in terms of the defined and undefined signs, and that
preferably take the form of equations involving numerical quantification; and a set of theorems each of which is derived from
one or more of the above principles and the explicitly stated
antecedent conditions.[12]

Hull goes on to argue that "the soundness, validity, or truth
of the postulates," and indirectly of the definitions of the terms
used in their formulation, is to be judged by "the conformity
of the deduced theorems to the observed outcome of the antecedent conditions." When such confirmation is not obtained,
either there was an error in deduction, or one of the primary
postulates was wrong; the latter error in turn may be the result
of a faulty definition. He then draws the moral that *"definitions
are capable of progressive empirical rectification and validation."*[13] Such a view of the empirical corrigibility of the use of
terms is quite different from the view often adopted by philosophic value theorists, who tend to start from a "correct" use of a
term and regard that as a precondition for further inquiry. In
my opinion, the scientific approach is far more fruitful, and the
self-correcting aspect of scientific inquiry should apply to the
use of terms as much as to anything else.

Hull then moves to an account of his natural science theory
of value. He takes valuating behavior as highly important and
as centrally involved in behavior in general: "any fairly detailed
and sound dynamic theory of behavior must ... necessarily con-

---

12*Ibid.*, pp. 126-127.
13*Ibid.*, pp. 127-128.

tain a theory of value regardless of whether the term 'value' appears in the system or not." A basic notion in his behavioral value theory is *primary need.* Hull does not attempt to give a complete account of this notion, but gives as a "rough elucidation":

> "The term 'primary need' represents those states or conditions of organisms, such as tissue injury, lack of food, water, optimal temperature, exercise, sleep, and sexual activity which if continued and/or intensified would tend to endanger the survival of the organism or the species."[14]

He goes on to say that one of his principles or postulates assumes that the organism, when in the condition of primary need, will "naturally" engage in a more or less random sequence of acts that either individually or in some combination may effect a reduction in need. Another postulate is that when an action is followed promptly by a need reduction, the organism will become appropriately conditioned; i.e., in the future a similar stimulus will evoke a similar reaction given similar circumstances. This "reaction potential" is taken by Hull to be a numerical value on a centigrade scale and is represented by '$_sE_R$'. When a group of stimuli tend to generate several incompatible reaction potentials at the same time, only the strongest will be evoked. But because of the "oscillation" of reaction potentials, an organism may react to a specific situation with different responses at different times.

'Striving' is introduced in the system as a "secondary or derived concept," and names the conversion of reaction potential into action by the "joint operation of stimulation and need." Need reduction often does not occur until several distinguishable actions are performed. The need reduction is called the 'primary goal,' and the results from the anterior acts of the series are called 'secondary' or 'subordinate' goals. These secondary goals sometimes function as reinforcement stimuli; the absence of secondary reinforcing states of affairs may give rise to striving even when the relevant primary need is not active. The lack or absence of a secondary goal is called a 'secondary need.' After the first

---

[14]*Ibid.*, p. 128.

few months of life, some species, especially the human, develop
behavioral patterns that for the most part are motivated by
secondary needs.[15]

Hull then moves to a specific treatment of "internal" states
that some believe can only be handled through introspection.
He holds that introspective reports are not useful when it comes
to measuring the *amount* of valuative behavior, but says this *"is
not primarily due to the fact that these introspections are private;
it arises because they cannot be precisely quantified."* But yet,
he says, such internal states can be treated quantitatively. The
natural science approach to the quantitative determination of
internal conditions concerning habit strength and motivation
proceeds "exactly as in the determination of many physical
values not easily measurable directly." He mentions velocity
and momentum as examples:

> "Velocity ordinarily is not itself directly measured. Never-
> theless it is neither private nor indeterminate. Velocity in the
> case of uniform motion is defined as the distance traversed by an
> object divided by the duration of the movement in question, the
> measurement of the distance and time ordinarily being separate
> public operations. In an exactly similar manner, momentum is
> a quantitative symbolic construct. It is the product of the mass
> of an object multiplied by its velocity, each of which may be
> determined by a separate public operation. Under certain cir-
> cumstances, such as those involved in the falling of a body, both
> velocity and momentum can be completely calculated in advance
> of the event from a knowledge of the value of gravity (g) at the
> point in question and the duration (t) of the fall from rest."[16]

What he calls "excitory potential" or "reaction potential"
($_sE_R$) is quantitatively anchored in a similar, although more
complicated, manner to measurable conditions. Examples of
such *antecedent* conditions are the number of reinforcements of
the action, the degree of need reduction produced in each reinforcement, the degree of similarity between the actual stimulus
and the stimuli involved in the original reinforcement, the magni-

---

[15]*Ibid.*, pp. 128-129.
[16]*Ibid.*, p. 130.

tude of the drive at the time the reaction was evoked, etc. On the *consequent* side, the intensity of the behavior resulting from the evoking stimulation, and many other aspects of the situation, are also measurable. He concludes:

> ". . . the potential striving of an organism is no more private or indeterminate than is the potential velocity or momentum of a kilogram of lead when it has fallen twenty feet from rest. . . . If the lead could talk as it falls, or if an articulate person were falling, the issue might be a little confused for scholars handicapped by certain types of metaphysical training, but the solution of the relevant equations would not be changed in the slightest degree."[17]

Although, to use the terminology proposed by Dewey and Bentley, Hull's approach throughout is much more interactional than transactional, in his discussion of the "paradox of the locus of value" Hull introduces a somewhat transactional way of viewing the problem. He takes the paradox as involving whether a value is located in the valued object or in the valuing organism. He says:

> "In a certain sense the question is a false one in that it implies that the locus must lie exclusively in one or the other. It is a little like asking whether the momentum of a falling object is due primarily to its mass or to the time it has been falling; the fact is that a knowledge of *both* is indispensable for the determination. The habit strength ($_sH_R$) *resides* in the state of the nervous system of the organism. This, in turn, *results* from a certain historical relationship between the organism and the object, situation, or state of affairs which has value such that the former has learned through reinforcement to strive for the latter. The actual striving results from the joint action of this internal condition and the stimulation arising in the situation."[18]

He further notes that the reinforcing characteristic of an object could be said to constitute the 'value,' as distinguished

---

[17]*Ibid.,* p. 131.
[18]*Ibid.,* pp. 131-132.

from 'valuation,' but that whether or not a given thing will serve as a reinforcement depends on the characteristics of the organism; although hay will reduce the food need of an ox, it will not reduce the food need of a human. So here too a roughly transactional approach is taken.

Finally, Hull considers verbal reports of "internal conditions," and argues that they are often useful. For example, in a clinical situation the patient's verbal reports may be helpful if time is too short to make exact calculations about "relevant habit structures" (assuming the availability of a complete enough history and the appropriate equations). According to Hull, introspective reports in general are useful for rough qualitative purposes, but they are less adequate in principle than quantitative laws.

E.   CRITICISM OF HULL

Hull's paper provides an interesting account of many of the things that need to be discussed if one hopes to develop a value theory in which values are scientifically measurable. Although I disagree with many of Hull's statements about science in general and psychology in particular, I regard his emphasis on ascertaining the most scientifically useful referents for terminology as highly important. I thoroughly agree with his insistence on changing the referent as further evidence becomes available. I also think Hull is correct in believing that his approach to valuating behavior permits many of the essential features of that behavior to be measured. As Hull also emphasizes, there are enormous practical problems in actually carrying out such measurements, but their feasibility in general seems reasonably established.

With the foregoing in mind, I would like to focus on three aspects of Hull's work.

(1) Although I think his account of natural science methodology is far too formal and relies too much on certain developments in physics, taking a more contextualist approach is still compatible with much of what Hull says. The important link between the two approaches is Hull's insistence that both the

"deduced theorems" and (indirectly) the adequacy of the uses of key terms are to be appraised in terms of observable outcomes. His empiricism in that respect makes his insistence that the structure of scientific theories should resemble the structure of formal logic (beginning with "undefined" signs, etc.) less dangerous than it otherwise would be. I am not here attempting to establish a view other than Hull's but simply pointing out that one could differ with his statement of the structure of a scientific theory and still find great merit in his views on value.

(2) Accepting for the moment something like Hull's account of how scientific terms may be progressively "rectified," we face the question of how close what he takes as valuational behavior is to what we ordinarily refer to in value discourse. Although Hull does not discuss that point directly, it seems clear enough that he takes *striving* as central to valuational behavior. Hull almost certainly would be among the first to insist that many people use value terminology in a different way, but I think he would also argue that the behavioral settings in which we normally say valuations are being made do involve striving as a central feature.

Since he views that kind of process as a most important one for behavior in general, he takes it as worthy of intensive investigation. Presumably he would not fight to the death to label that behavior as 'valuation,' if others refused to use terminology the same way. What he seems to be saying is that such behavior is highly significant, is intimately involved with what we often take as valuational behavior, and is amenable to a thoroughly scientific treatment. If some other use of the term 'value' could offer similar but greater advantages, probably he would be happy to revise his terminology.

(3) Assuming that Hull has focused attention on behavioral processes that are closely and essentially related to value phenomena, an important question concerns the most appropriate framework for studying those phenomena. My main differences with Hull occur on this issue. My strategy will be to show that some of the problems generated by Hull's approach are minimized or do not occur if a more transactional approach is taken. This is not, of course, equivalent to refuting Hull's approach

or to establishing a transactional approach, but will serve both
to illuminate some important issues and to suggest some evidence
in favor of transactionalism.

Let us start with the distinction between primary and secondary needs. In harmony with many other psychologists, Hull
works this distinction quite hard, although he clearly states that
for humans (and other higher mammalian organisms) behavior
after infancy "is for the most part motivated by secondary needs."
Along with the primary-secondary distinction goes a fairly sharp
differentiation between the organism and its environment; in
short, an interactional framework is adopted in which presumed
separates are brought together in various ways. Interactionism
can be contrasted to the transactional framework, which among
psychologists is often called a "biosocial" approach.

The biosocial approach regards needs as outcomes of
organism-environment instabilities and relations rather than as
instabilities *within* the organism as an isolated entity. The help
of other humans is often required in satisfying needs, and so
need satisfactions are social. "Primary" needs are not always
"prepotent"; some individuals choose to starve rather than to
give up the satisfaction of acquired or derived needs.[19] These
issues are discussed in more detail in Chapter VIII, Section G.

If needs are biosocial, a theoretical approach emphasizing
the satisfaction of primary needs may generate problems. In
Hull's framework, for example, striving that results from "secondary reinforcement" produces what he describes as a paradox
that is not easily resolved. He takes as a classical case the
chimpanzees studied by J. B. Wolfe. In experimental situations
the chimpanzees could get poker chips that later could be put
in a slot machine and would deliver a grape for each chip. Hull
says:

> "Since the chimpanzee strives for the poker chip, it may
> properly be said that the chip is valued. However, since the chip
> has no capacity to reduce a primary need, it may be said to have

---

[19]See, for example, Patrick Mullahy, "A Philosophy of Personality," in Howard
Brand, ed., *The Study of Personality*, New York, Wiley, 1954, p. 51; Norman Cameron,
The Psychology of Behavior Disorders, Boston, Houghton Mifflin, 1947, pp. 104-105,
pp. 126-127; Handy, *op. cit.*, Chapter VII.

no intrinsic value. But since it is an indispensable *means* to the securing of grapes, which do reduce the primary need for food, the poker chip has an indirect but genuine value. It is a subordinate goal and as such possesses secondary reinforcing powers."[20]

But if, as Hull himself insists, most higher mammalian behavior involves satisfying secondary rather than primary needs, why call the securing of chips an "indirect" value and relegate it to a secondary status? To hold that the chimpanzee strives for the chips in order sometime in the future to get a grape may be correct, but is inferential enough so that other possibilities should be kept in mind. Possibly in some such instances there is a curiosity need that is satisfied by winning the poker chip, and the striving is better related to that than to some future satiation of hunger. A graduate student in psychology I once knew was working on an experiment with monkeys in which the reward for solving a puzzle was a bit of food. The whole experimental design was predicated on the notion of controlling the food deprivation of the monkeys, and their motivation for working the puzzle was assumed to be the food. But to the student's chagrin the monkeys often failed to eat their food although they "worked hard" at the problem, and indeed seemed far less interested in the reward than in solving the problem. Behavior may be more complex than is assumed in a particular experimental design.

A transactional approach also avoids some of the difficulties about the "locus of value": is value in the object strived for, or in the valuing organism? As noted, Hull's approach to this problem does approximate a transactional approach. The apparent paradox disappears when attention and analysis are directed to the process as a whole. Then, as aspects or phases of the transaction, one can focus on the object that satisfies a need, or on the need, or on something else, as appropriate. By not assuming "separates" in the first place, there is no logical or epistemological problem of bringing them together, and as long as the entire process is held in view, provisional focusing on differentiable aspects or phases may be productive.

Looking at these matters another way, a transactional ap-

---

[20]Hull, *op. cit.*, p. 132.

proach has the advantage of viewing a "dynamic" field of events and following the dynamics to a natural conclusion. Roughly speaking, in the case of need satisfaction some tension or instability in behavior generates activity that normally leads to a satisfaction of the need. Mistakes may occur in that some of the objects "tried out" will not satisfy the need, or will only do so inefficiently. When the need is satisfied, equilibrium is reestablished. Within such a dynamic process, the various aspects and phases of the process can be viewed in relation to each other without generating methodogenic problems that have little or nothing to do with the empirical process being studied.

Hull also discusses an instance in which something (X) that will *not* reduce a need chances to be quite similar to something (Y) that previously has reduced that need. X will evoke striving activity, but should we say it has value? After X has evoked a few striving reactions, the organism will cease to strive for it, but will continue to strive for Y. Hull holds that we could say that X has no value for the organism, but still that the organism values it for a time. Although I have no strong objection to Hull's approach here, I think it would be simpler to account for what is observed in terms of a valuing transaction. Just because a human, say, incorrectly believes X will satisfy a need does not generate a value paradox; it simply shows that an organism can make mistakes about what will satisfy its needs, or can confuse an X with a Y.

Finally, in principle I agree fully with Hull that the various aspects and phases of striving behavior can be measured, and also that in practice carrying out the measurements may be difficult and time consuming. His approach has the merit of not postulating entities or processes that theoretically cannot be measured.

F.   CONCLUSION

Although major attention in this chapter has been focused on the work of only two psychologists, the issues raised have many implications for current work in value measurement.

Among those who think values can be measured scientifically, two important subgroups can be distinguished. The first group, represented by Thurstone, proceeds by getting oral or pencil-and-paper responses from the subjects to a set of fixed questions, and relies on introspection. The second group, represented by Hull, hopes to measure values without much reliance on that type of response and instead urges a direct study of striving behavior.

However, much of the controversy about introspective reports, internal states, etc., is wide of the mark. The questionnaire techniques do not necessarily get at the subject's introspective states at all (whatever they may be) but in fact are inquiries into what the subject *says* about those states, which is a form of observable behavior. Nor does a theoretically possible measurement of, say, "the degree of need reduction involved in each reinforcement" necessarily get at any internal state of the organism purely and simply; how much need reduction occurs often depends as much on the environment and the social setting as it does on anything within the organism.

I have argued that the appropriate thing to say about all the types of measurement under consideration is that various types of behavior are being investigated.[21] Doubtless there are enormous differences in the scientific successes of those various measurements, but for the moment let us ignore that. We are faced with a variety of different investigative techniques that lead to warranted results about various aspects of human behavior. What we need to emphasize more than sometimes is done is which of those aspects we want to label 'value.' If that can be decided, then we are in a position to ask intelligently which of the available techniques does the best job of measuring values so construed. From the above point of view, I believe we are in a position to sum up some of the general difficulties of value measurement.

One of the main reasons why questionnaire approaches are so often used is that relatively quick and inexpensive responses

---

[21]Here as elsewhere in this book, the emphasis on inquiry into *behavior* should not be misunderstood as an acceptance of any particular form of psychological *behaviorism*. Many behaviorisms postulate a far narrower view of behavior than here adopted and construe behavior as located entirely within the organism.

can be obtained with techniques now at hand. The difficulty is that it is not easy to assess how close the results of such inquiry are to whatever it is that is taken as value. Assume for a moment that need satisfaction is taken as basic to value. If so, are those filling out the questionnaires fully aware of what would satisfy their needs, are they likely to give honest answers to the inquirer, etc.? Or assume that preference is taken as basic to value. Despite the increasing sophistication and cleverness of questionnaires, how sure are we that the preferences so expressed will conform to the preferences of the same person as observed "naturalistically"? In short, as mentioned, whenever the basic situation is one in which a subject says what his response would be under hypothetical conditions, there are possibilities of error.

On the other hand, the "firmer" mode of measurement proposed by Hull faces the problem that at present we are not very well able to measure what his theory calls for measuring. The by-passing of the problems involved in a subject's saying what his response would be under hypothetical conditions offers theoretical advantages, but at present those advantages may be more than offset by other difficulties.

My major complaint against many who are working on the measurement of values is *not* that they have failed to make more progress than they have, but rather that too often the difficulties are glossed over or are ignored. Questionnaire constructors, for example, can check on the internal consistency of a respondent's answers about his preferences in ingenious ways, but then sometimes cite that consistency as evidence that the choices the person says he would make are the same as the actual choices that would be made in appropriate circumstances. Or the "hard-science" people, while admitting their present inability to make some of the measurements that their theory requires, cite the theoretical possibility of such measurement as though that solved all the problems.

Many of the issues just mentioned will be considered again in different perspectives in later chapters. My position is that we should focus on valuing transactions; when that is done, we find a great many aspects or phases of the transaction that are worth further detailed study. The precise techniques used to measure the various aspects may vary considerably. I am not suggesting that we should eliminate questionnaires, nor am I casting doubt on their usefulness; for many purposes they may give us just the information we want in a reliable form. What we should not do, however, is to confuse what has been achieved in questionnaire studies with something else. (A main difficulty seems to be the open or disguised assumption that an inner, subjective, nonphysical mind does something, and that something can be gotten at through questionnaires.) At the same time, I think that the natural science approach to value measurement offers great promise, and indeed may some day produce just the type of warranted information that will make questionnaire studies even more useful than they are at present. But such future pots of gold should not be mistaken for already achieved results.

Or, putting this another way, even what seems to be the poorer work on value measurement may have some significance if greater clarity can be achieved about just what is measured and the range of the findings. The vagueness about what values are, combined with a rosy optimism that the results of a given investigation have a greater range of application than they do have, may lead to a foolish exaggeration of achievements.

Chapter IV

SOME SOCIAL PSYCHOLOGICAL STUDIES
OF VALUES

A. OVERVIEW

Some fairly typical attempts of psychologists and sociologists to measure values will be examined in this chapter. Looking at the kind of work that is being done will help illuminate some of the questions in measurement theory discussed earlier and also show that at least some of the questions raised by philosophers in the latter part of this book are pertinent. In the present chapter, consideration will be given to the Allport-Vernon-Lindzey Study of Values, to William Catton's attempt to show that qualitatively unlike values are quantitatively commensurable, to the F Scale developed in *The Authoritarian Personality*, and to Roy E. Carter's use of the "Koloman" procedure to study the relative importance of certain social values.

B. THE ALLPORT-VERNON-LINDZEY STUDY OF VALUES

The well-known *Study of Values*[1] is subtitled *A Scale for Measuring the Dominant Interests in Personality*. It was original-ly published in 1931, and has been widely used. The scale is intended "to measure the relative prominence of six basic in-

---

[1]Gordon W. Allport, Philip E. Vernon, and Gardner Lindzey, *Study of Values*, 3rd ed., Boston, Houghton Mifflin, 1960. This is a nineteen page manual.

terests or motives in personality;" the six interests were derived from Eduard Spranger's *Types of Men*. Spranger, who argued that an individual's personality is best investigated through an inquiry into the person's values or evaluative attitudes, discussed the following "ideal types" of man:

(1) *The Theoretical.* The dominant interest of this ideal type is discovering the truth. His aim is to systematize and order knowledge without regard to the beauty or utility of objects, but only on a "cognitive" basis. Scientists and philosophers typify this category. (Spranger's classification was based not on *achievements* within any of the categories, but rather on the person's interests and intentions, so even a poor scientist could exemplify this particular ideal type.)

(2) *The Economic.* Here the dominant interest is in the useful, and a business man would exemplify the category. The economic man insists that education should be practical and is suspicious of unapplied knowledge.

(3) *The Aesthetic.* The highest value for this ideal type is found in form and harmony. Life is seen as a procession of events, each of which is to be enjoyed for its own sake.

(4) *The Social.* Here the dominant value is love of people. Other humans are prized as ends; the social man is unselfish and sympathetic.

(5) *The Political.* Here the focus is on power; leaders in almost any field fall into this category. The political man wants direct personal power, influence, etc.

(6) *The Religious.* The basic value here is unity. The religious man tends to be a mystic and wants to comprehend the entire cosmos.

The original version of the Allport-Vernon-Lindzey scale was closely based on Spranger's six types, but in the revised form the social value was modified on the ground that Spranger's approach produced low reliability. The authors felt that Spranger's notion of the social was too broad, for it included love in any form, and so in their revised scale love was restricted to altruistic love or philanthropy. The authors also point out that Spranger holds "a somewhat flattering view of human nature," since he does not allow for "formless or valueless personalities" or for primarily hedonistic individuals. In addition, Spranger neglects the "sheerly sensuous values." The authors say that to the extent their scale neglects the "baser" values and those that "are not permitted to reach the level of conscious choice," the neglect is due to following Spranger's formulations.

The Allport-Vernon-Lindzey scale is designed for college students or adults who have had some college education. It is self-scoring, may be taken individually or in a group setting, and has no time limit. The authors caution against letting the subjects "know too much" about the six basic values before they take the test.

The test consists of two Parts. In Part I, either of two possible alternative answers can be selected. For example, one item asks which of two fields of study the subject expects will ultimately be most important for man, and the alternative answers are mathematics and theology. Another question asks whether you would rather be a banker or a politician, assuming that you had the ability to be either. The respondent has a total of 3 points to distribute between the two alternatives. If he prefers a) to b), he gives 3 points to a) and 0 points to b). If he prefers b) to a), the reverse is done. If he has only a slight preference for one alternative, that is given 2 points and the other is given 1 point.

In Part II, four alternative answers to each question are provided. For example, respondents are asked if they would prefer to be a mathematician, a sales manager, a clergyman, or a politician, assuming they had the necessary abilities and the salaries were identical. Another question asks which of the following famous people most interests the respondent: Florence Nightingale, Napoleon, Henry Ford, or Galileo. In this part of the test, the alternative of highest preference is given 4 points, the next 3 points, the next 2 points, and the lowest preference is given 1 point.

In both parts of the test, the points must be assigned in the manner described, but if the respondent finds it impossible to indicate a preference, the question can be omitted. When the scores are totalled for the whole test, on omitted questions equal scores are allocated to each of the alternatives.

In all there are 120 alternatives, 20 of which refer to each of the six values. The totals for each value are added. After applying some simple corrections, the totals for each of the six values are plotted on a profile. A subject having a profile that is nearly flat favors all six values nearly equally. The test does not "measure the absolute strength of each of the six values, but only their *relative* strength," so a high score on one value is obtainable only if a lower score is achieved on one or more of the remaining values. The test was constructed so that a score of 40 is the average for each value. The authors say:

> "In interpreting the results, therefore, it is necessary to bear in mind that they reveal only the *relative* importance of each of the six values in a given personality, not the total amount of 'value energy' or motivation possessed by an individual. It is quite possible for the highest value of a generally apathetic person to be less intense and effective than the lowest value of a person in whom all values are prominent and dynamic."[2]

The test was standardized on a college population, nearly all of whom were in a liberal arts program. Much work has been done to help assure reliability (i.e., that similar results will be obtained when the test is repeated). On validation (i.e., that the test measures what it is supposed to measure), the authors maintain that the most direct and convincing support is the examination of scores for groups with known characteristics. "Common experience," they say, makes us expect that on the average women will be more *religious, social,* and *aesthetic* than men, and engineering students would be expected to rate high on *theoretical* and *economic* values. Such expectations are borne out by the scores.

Among the uses suggested for the test are the areas of counseling and vocational guidance. In such settings, the counselor can use the test to get an initial notion of the client's interests. The authors emphasize that the test is intended primarily for subjects who want to cooperate with the examiner in order to find out

[2]*Ibid.,* p. 8.

more about their interests and values. When it is suspected that the subjects do not want an "honest" picture of themselves, the test should be used with great caution or not at all.

C.   COMMENTARY ON ALLPORT-VERNON-LINDZEY SCALE

In a variety of important ways the *Study of Values* illustrates some of the problems encountered in alleged measurements of values. First, there are a whole series of technical or "internal" questions that could be raised. For convenience, reference here will be made to just one review of the test and relevant literature.[3] Gage describes the test as "very good," and says it gives the impression "of being an intelligent test for intelligent people." However, he raises questions about the 1951 revision, and says that the correlations between the old form and the revised form are low enough "to call for revalidation of the test." He further is critical of the data used for comparison of internal consistency and repeat reliabilities, and says that if "reliability is worth taking seriously, it deserves less cavalier treatment."

Gage also raises a question about the system (in the revised version) of writing responses directly in the test booklet, which simplifies the totalling of the scores. He suggests that this procedure could make the test even more transparent than it was, and says that a college student may have little trouble in discerning which of the alternatives represent the same value: "If he wants to fake, he gets a helping hand from this arrangement." Since the authors stressed that the subject must want to be "honest," one wonders how honest the respondents actually are, especially at a time in which respondents may have increasing sophistication about tests and the uses to which the results might be put.

As a final sample of the possible "internal" problems raised by Gage, he notes that in Part I the respondent can respond either with a 3–0 degree of intensity or a 2–1 degree. Gage is "willing to predict that reliable individual differences" will be found as to which mode of responding about "intensity" will be made, and

---

[3]The review by N. L. Gage, *Fifth Mental Measurements Yearbook*, 1959, pp. 199-202.

says that this "stylistic variable" may be relevant to the subject's values.

Without pursuing such matters further, it is safe to say that even in widely used and respected tests of this sort important "internal" problems can occur. For our purposes, however, "external" questions may be of even greater significance.

First, we may ask what is putatively being measured. As the title indicates, the answer is "values." But the subtitle suggests that "dominant personality interests" is the answer. And the first sentence of a *Study of Values* refers to six basic "interests or motives in personality." All of these terms ('value,' 'interest,' 'motive') are used somewhat loosely. Some critics have objected that the scale confounds what should be distinguished—*values* and *interests*—on the ground that a militant atheist, for example, may be keenly interested in religion although maintaining that religion has little value. On the other hand, some value theorists attempt to define 'value' in terms of 'interest,' and distinguish between negative and positive interests (and thus values.)[4] We simply cannot discuss intelligently what any given test does or does not measure until we understand what the referents are for the key terms.

What does seem to have been measured (in a sense) is the relative degree of preference a respondent indicates he has for six different clusters of alternatives. If this is a fair statement of what is being done, several questions immediately arise. Why those six clusters, based on Spranger, and not others? Since the authors were willing to revise one of Spranger's categories, and insist that his typology is somewhat defective, why not make further changes? Why call the clusters 'value'? A hostile critic might suspect that term was chosen simply because it is so vague yet honorific. And, what guarantee, if any, do we have that even honest respondents understand what is being asked for in the same way when they are told to mark their preferences?

For example, one question asks whether the magazine *Scientific Age* or *Arts and Decorations* would be chosen by the respondent if only those two were available in a waiting room.

4For example, see my discussion of R. B. Perry's general theory of value in Ch. VII.

Which answer is selected may correspond to the magazine that would be read in that situation, or might instead reflect the "self-image" the respondent would like to have, or something else. I do not wish to deny that it is useful to find out about "self-images" in contrast to other forms of behavior, and I am not saying that there is necessarily anything greatly wrong with the way the test is set up. The point I wish to make is that there can be important differences among various behavioral situations in which preferences are expressed; brief questions may be responded to with quite different assumptions on the part of the respondent about what is wanted.

The main caution I want to suggest is that (contrary to what might be assumed) the *Study of Values* does not measure all, or all the most important, values (however understood) an individual has, but rather gives a relative measure of the preferences an individual says he has from among six groupings.

D. CATTON AND THE QUANTITATIVE COMMENSURABILITY OF VALUES

Catton, following somewhat along the lines suggested by George A. Lundberg, is interested in the techniques that can be used for measuring human values.[5] In discussing "value patterns," Catton mentions the "ends desired" by a group, the conditions under which those ends are desired, and the "relative intensity" with which they are desired, so it seems evident that Catton takes desires as fundamental to values. He goes on to discuss why social scientists have tended to avoid inquiry into values, and suggests part of the answer is that often both philosophers and social scientists assume or argue that qualitatively unlike values are not quantitatively commensurable. His aim is to devise some empirical tests of the hypothesis that qualitatively unlike values are not commensurable. He discusses three such tests.

---

[5]William R. Catton, Jr., "Exploring Techniques for Measuring Human Values," *American Sociological Review*, Vol. 19, 1954.

The first relies upon data from the *American Soldier* series.[6] The data concern a survey relating to the "point system" for establishing the order in which World War II soldiers would be demobilized. The survey dealt with four items: length of time in service, age, overseas duty, and dependents. The respondents (U. S. soldiers) were asked, for each possible pair of those four items, which should be given the heaviest weight in determining when a soldier would be discharged. Stouffer describes such choices as comparing the relative importance of "battles and babies."

Catton argues that such items seem to be qualitatively dissimilar and thus, on some theories, to be quantitatively incommensurable. He argues that if qualitative dissimilarity does in fact interfere with co-measuring, the preference responses should tend to be random when all possible pairs are presented. But if commensurability exists, then a hierarchical pattern among the responses should occur. (I. e., one item would have a preference assignment of 3, another of 2, another of 1, and none for the fourth, indicating that the most important item was more important than any of the other three, the second most important was more important than two others, but less important than the first, etc.) Stouffer reported that over 90% of his respondents did produce such a hierarchical pattern. After statistical analysis, Catton says: "we may conclude with reasonable confidence that, in the minds of World War II American soldiers, such values as battles and babies were not incommensurable."

His second test concerned new data. Members of two introductory sociology classes were tested in relation to five desiderata that were said to be equally priced ($2.00 each), and which were thought by the experimenter to be qualitatively different from each other: a ticket to a concert, a steak dinner, a ticket to a ball game, a pair of gloves, and a carton of cigarettes. The respondents were asked on a questionnaire to indicate how qualitatively similar or dissimilar they thought each possible pair of items was, and also to indicate which of each pair was preferred. (Preference was

---

[6]Samuel A. Stouffer, *et al.*, *The American Soldier: Combat and its Aftermath*, Princeton, Princeton University Press, 1949, pp. 521-522.

expressed in three ways: which the respondent would "walk farthest to get," which he would "act quickest to get," and which he would be most willing "to miss class to get." The different ways produced such similar results that only the "walk farthest" data were used.)

The degree of qualitative dissimilarity, as judged by the respondents, was considerable. When the preferences were analyzed, the hierarchical ordering was prominent, and on the basis of statistical treatment, Catton says that "with fair confidence it can be concluded that the five rather dissimilar desiderata used in the experiment are not incommensurable."

He then observes that since the desiderata in the experiment just cited are rather trivial, other values of a higher order of abstraction, and perhaps of significance, should be studied. He refers to an earlier study in which Thorndike mentioned "infinitely strong" wants. The desideratum for such a want is "utterly desirable" and is thus not "a quantity to be weighed in comparison with others." Catton also refers to some comments by Brand Blanshard about the dilemma of "absolute pacifists" at the time the Japanese invaded Manchuria. Those pacifists were opposed to the use of force against Japan, but yet believed that if the Japanese were not compelled to obey international law there would be even more violence and a greater cost in human life. According to Blanshard, such pacifists often became "helpless, hurt and bewildered," since they had to "balance infinites against each other."[7]

In trying to see if even "infinite" values might be commensurable, Catton thought a population in which 'infinite' was an everyday word was desirable, and so he chose Protestant clergymen. He asked a sample of clergymen to list the values "which they thought were *of infinite worth to human beings.*" Only about one-fourth of the sample complied, but from their responses Catton settled on six "abstract values" which he believed sub-

---

[7]E. L. Thorndike, "Valuations of Certain Pains, Deprivations, and Frustrations," *Journal of Genetic Psychology,* Vol. 51, 1937, pp. 235-236. Brand Blanshard, "Theology and the Value of the Individual," in *The Scientific Spirit and Democratic Faith,* New York, King's Crown Press, 1944, pp. 84-85.

sumed practically everything suggested by the respondents. The six values were: 1) Human life itself; 2) Man's creative achievements; 3) Wholesome cooperation with our fellow men for a happier life for all; 4) Worship of God and acceptance of God's will; 5) Fullest development of the moral character of mankind; 6) Fullest development of human intelligence and human abilities.

Three questionnaire forms were constructed. One presented the six values in paired comparisons, another asked that the six values be ranked, and the third that the respondent indicate which of the six values were of infinite worth. Each of the six values was in fact designated by some respondents as being of infinite worth. As in the case of the two earlier experiments, here again the respondents did discriminate between the relative worth of the different items. According to Catton:

> "From such evidence it seems reasonable to infer one of two things: (1) that 'infinite' values can be measured according to established scaling techniques, or else (2) that clergymen are a bit unrigorous in their use of the term 'infinite' (that is, they do not use it in a sense comparable to its mathematical meaning). In a way these are merely two phrasings of the same inference."[8]

It is interesting to note that some of the respondents protested and indicated on the questionnaire forms that they felt somewhat "helpless, hurt and bewildered" when asked to rate such items comparatively, but they still went ahead and did so. Catton's general conclusion is that "human values. . . become measurable relative to each other in exactly the same manner as other verbal stimuli—by application of Thurstone's law of comparative judgment."

E.   COMMENTARY ON CATTON'S WORK

Quite often in discussions of value theory, the statement *is* made that certain values are incommensurable with other values, and I think Catton has shown that at least some interpretations

---

[8]Catton, *op. cit.*, p. 54.

of that statement are mistaken. Indeed, I would go so far as to suggest that often those who discuss in the abstract the incommensurability of values simply have little idea of what they are talking about in the first place; in their zeal to "protect" values against a scientific treatment they indulge in remarks that make little or no sense. One suspects that something similar is involved on the part of some who emphasize "infinite" values, for they either do not mean that values are literally infinite or else they inconsistently go ahead and make comparative judgments anyway.

Looking at this in another way, a common phenomenon is the differential allocation of resources among things that in some sense are qualitatively quite different. In our society, we constantly have to choose whether to spend money on food, or clothing, or housing, and it is clear that these three items are quite different and are hardly interchangeable in function. But they are commensurable in the sense that we unhesitatingly allocate our income differentially to them. And similar considerations apply to the allocation of time we give to qualitatively dissimilar items, such as eating and going to a concert. In short, a characteristic feature of human life is that different kinds of things are judged as commensurable for the purpose of allocating available resources. Indeed, according to R. B. Perry, the problem in assessing values is not in their incommensurability, but rather in their commensurability. (See Chapter VII, Section C.)

Of course, it may be possible for someone to so use the term 'value' that qualitatively dissimilar values are incommensurable. So again we are back at our old problem: what is the referent for 'value'? To apply this to the preceding remarks, the various qualitatively different items mentioned might all be considered as kinds of satisfaction (of a need or interest). Assuming for the moment that satisfaction is central to value, is the value that which satisfies, or is it the process of satisfying, or the resulting quiescence, or some combination of those factors, or something else? Whether or in what sense values are commensurable depends somewhat on such issues.

At this point it may be useful to refer to a later article by

Catton.[9] He begins by saying that a 'desideratum' is anything desired by someone at some time. He goes on to say: " 'Valuing' may then be defined as actions which show a person's intensity of desire for various desiderata." He further says that when inquiring into the values of a person or a group "a sociologist studies 'inferential constructs,' rather than directly observable phenomena." Such constructs do not always resemble verbal statements, but may be inferences from the choices of persons or groups. Then, after discussing the work of some other scholars, he modifies the view of Clyde Kluckhohn to arrive at the following: *"A value is a conception of the desirable which is implied by a set of preferential responses to symbolic desiderata."*[10]

These comments raise, of course, the issue of the relation of what is desired in fact by an individual, what he regards as desirable even if he does not select it, and what is desirable for that individual even if he does not recognize it, and how best to relate values to those possibilities. That topic is discussed elsewhere in this book, so I will not go into it now.

What I wish to point out is that Catton takes a stand in favor of studying something that is symbolic, or a construct, or a verbal statement, rather than "directly observable phenomena." Just what the difference is between a "directly observable phenomenon" and, say, a verbal stimulus, is not clear to me, for the latter seems as directly observable as anything else. In a skeptical mood one might suspect that those who specify 'value' in terms of 'symbolic desiderata' or 'verbal stimuli' do so partly because of their penchant for questionnaire studies. In any event, I agree with Catton when he says: "Compliance of behavior with stated norms, or consistency between operative values and conceived values, must be discovered empirically, rather than assumed *a priori*."[11] (I do not, of course, intend to say that a "stated norm" is not part of behavior.)

---

[9]William R. Catton, Jr., "A Theory of Value," *American Sociological Review*, Vol. 24, 1959.

[10]*Ibid.*, p. 312.

[11]*Ibid.*

F. THE AUTHORITARIAN PERSONALITY

In contrast to the work mentioned so far in this book, that done in the project now to be described[12] puts much emphasis on those factors of which the person is not consciously aware. Although the F Scale (Fascism Scale), which will be our major topic of consideration, is not labelled simply or exclusively as a measure of value, its content in many ways is similar to other scales behavioral scientists have developed under the rubric of value measurement. The book as a whole is a blending of psychoanalytic and academic psychological theory with empirical inquiry of the type often found in social psychological research.

In view of the overall aim of the volume, many decisions were made throughout the research that would be challenged by other workers. That, of course, is not said as a negative criticism, but only to point out that estimates of the achievements of the research are subject to a vast array of possible criticisms.

The authors state as a major hypothesis:

> ". . . that the political, economic, and social convictions of an individual often form a broad and coherent pattern, as if bound together by a 'mentality' or 'spirit,' and that this pattern is an expression of deep-lying trends in his personality."[13]

Their main concern was with people who were "potentially fascistic," or whose personality structures were likely to make them especially susceptible to antidemocratic propaganda. Such people "have a great deal in common," including a cluster of "opinions, attitudes, and values."

According to the authors, opinions, attitudes, and values are "expressed more or less openly in words," and in that sense are psychologically "on the surface." However, the degree of openness with which a person responds depends upon the context, especially in the case of sensitive issues such as those concern-

---

[12]T. W. Adorno, Else Frenkel-Brunswik, Daniel J. Levinson, and R. Nevitt Sanford, *The Authoritarian Personality*, New York, Harper & Row, 1950.

[13]*Ibid.*, p. 1.

ing current ideological debates, minority groups, etc. There may well be a difference between what a person says in a fairly public setting and what he will express confidentially to friends. But even the latter, the authors say, can be observed directly using appropriate psychological techniques. In addition, however, a person may have "secret" views that he almost never will reveal to anyone else, or thoughts that he cannot admit even to himself, or ideas that are so vague or ill-formed that he cannot put them into words. The authors say: "To gain access to these deeper trends is particularly important, for precisely here may lie the individual's potential for democratic or antidemocratic thought and action in crucial situations."[14]

All the aspects of an individual's attitudes, values, etc., are part of an organized structure that may contain contradictions and inconsistencies, but in which the constituents are "related in psychologically meaningful ways." To understand such a structure, a theory of the total personality is required. The authors took Freud's views as basic in working out their theory of personality structure, and were guided by academic psychologists in their attempt to formulate the "more directly observable and measurable aspects of personality."

The authors view personality as "a more or less enduring organization of forces within the individual." These "forces" help to determine a person's behavior, and help explain what consistency it has, but behavior is not viewed as the same thing as personality: "personality lies *behind* behavior and *within* the individual." The "forces" are not responses, but "readinesses for response," and are primarily needs that vary from one person to another in terms of quality, intensity, mode of gratification, etc. Since personality "is essentially an organization of needs," and opinions, attitudes, and values depend upon needs, personality is a *"determinant* of ideological preferences." However, the personality is not hypostatized as some ultimate determinant, and it is said to evolve in relation to the social environment.[15]

---

[14]*Ibid.,* p. 4.
[15]*Ibid.,* pp. 5-6.

In describing their general methodology, the authors say:

"A particular methodological challenge was imposed by the conception of *levels* in the person; this made it necessary to devise techniques for surveying opinions, attitudes, and values that were on the surface, for revealing ideological trends that were more or less inhibited and reached the surface only in indirect manifestations, and for bringing to light personality forces that lay in the subject's unconscious. And since the major concern was with *patterns* of dynamically related factors—something that requires study of the total individual—it seemed that the proper approach was through intensive clinical studies. The significance and practical importance of such studies could not be gauged, however, until there was knowledge of how far it was possible to generalize from them. Thus it was necessary to perform group studies as well as individual studies, and to find ways and means for integrating the two."[16]

Groups were studied through questionnaires, and individuals through interviews and clinical tests; both approaches were carried on in close conjunction. Clinical studies of an individual's underlying wishes, fears, defenses, etc., were used to help arrive at items for the group questionnaires, and the group studies helped show what opinions, attitudes, and values were associated together and their relation to life histories and the contemporary situations of individuals.

To help identify "potentially antidemocratic" individuals, a questionnaire was filled out by many people. Among other items, the questionnaire contained antidemocratic statements with which the respondent was asked to agree or disagree. Those who showed the greatest amount of agreement with such statements (and for control purposes, also those who showed most disagreement, and some who were neutral) were given psychiatric interviews and tested clinically through the use of the Thematic Apperception Test (TAT). The questionnaire was then revised in view of the clinical findings. The notion of validity here was to find questionnaire items that correlated highly with opinions people would express in the clinical situation.

[16]*Ibid.*, pp. 11-12.

Since it was assumed that many people would not be willing to speak frankly about the ideological issues the authors were trying to get at, the scale had to be constructed in a different way than those designed to measure only surface issues. The procedure was to bring together items in the scale that, on the basis of clinical experience and the authors' theories, were presumed to indicate trends lying "relatively deep" within the personality and which constituted a disposition either to express, or to be influenced by, fascistic ideas. In the main the questionnaire items were designed to serve as rationalizations for irrational tendencies.

To illustrate, two statements on the scale were (1) "Nowadays when so many different kinds of people move around so much and mix together so freely, a person has to be especially careful to protect himself against infection and disease," and (2) "Homosexuality is a particularly rotten form of delinquency and ought to be severely punished." Individuals who agreed with one of those statements tended to agree with the other, and also tended to agree with openly antidemocratic statements.

Questionnaires were collected from over 2,000 respondents. Many were college students, but also there were prison inmates, psychiatric patients, labor union members, Kiwanis Club members, etc. In general, most subjects were drawn from the middle socioeconomic class, and the inquirers found early in their study that somewhat different instruments and procedures would be necessary for subjects having a lower socioeconomic background. The authors say that the "findings of the study may be expected to hold fairly well for non-Jewish, white, native-born, middle-class Americans," but that their population is "rather inadequate" as a basis for generalizing about the total population of the U. S.[17]

In constructing the F scale, the authors hoped to develop an instrument that would measure prejudice without mentioning any minority group by name and without appearing to have the aim that it did have. By circumventing certain defenses an individual might use when asked directly about race issues, a better

---

[17]*Ibid.*, p. 23.

measure of prejudice could result. Each item in the scale was based on an hypothesis (or hypotheses) as to the item's connection with prejudice. These hypotheses in turn resulted from earlier research. The authors did not begin with hundreds of items chosen almost randomly and then find out which ones might be associated with what they wanted to measure, but rather began with items that were theoretically linked to potential facism.

The original F Scale was derived from the larger set of questionnaire items which the respondents answered. Nine different variables made up the basic content of the scale. Each such variable was regarded "as a more or less central trend in the person" which (according to the authors' view of personality dynamics) expresses itself in ethnocentric behavior.

Listed below are the nine variables, the brief description given of each, and a sample F Scale item:

1. *Conventionalism.* Rigid adherence to conventional, middleclass values. (A sample item is: One should avoid doing things in public which appear wrong to others, even though one knows that these things are really all right.)

2. *Authoritarian submission.* Submissive, uncritical attitude toward idealized moral authorities of the ingroup. (Every person should have a deep faith in some supernatural force higher than himself to which he gives a total allegiance and whose decisions he does not question.)

3. *Authoritarian aggression.* Tendency to be on the lookout for, and to condemn, reject, and punish people who violate conventional values. (Homosexuality is a particularly rotten form of delinquency and ought to be severely punished.)

4. *Anti-intraception.* Opposition to the subjective, the imaginative, the tender-minded. (There is too much emphasis in colleges on intellectual and theoretical topics, and not enough emphasis on practical matters and on the homely virtues of living.)

5. *Superstition and stereotypy.* The belief in mystical determinants of the individual's fate; the disposition to think in rigid categories. (Although many people may scoff, it may yet be shown that astrology can explain a lot of things.)

6. *Power and "toughness."* Preoccupation with the domi-

nance-submission, strong-weak, leader-follower dimension; identification with power figures; overemphasis upon the conventionalized attributes of the ego; exaggerated assertion of strength and toughness. (No insult to our honor should ever go unpunished.)

7. *Destructiveness and cynicism.* Generalized hostility, vilification of the human. (No matter how they act on the surface, men are interested in women for only one reason.)

8. *Projectivity.* The disposition to believe that wild and dangerous things go on in the world; the projection outwards of unconscious emotional impulses. (The sexual orgies of the old Greeks and Romans are nursery school stuff compared to some of the goings-on in this country today, even in circles where people might least expect it.)

9. *Sex.* Exaggerated concern with sexual "goings-on." (Sex crimes, such as rape and attacks on children, deserve more than mere imprisonment; such criminals ought to be publicly whipped.)[18] A single item may represent more than one of the variables, and the different variables are represented by different numbers of items; the main concern was the overall pattern in which the variables fitted.

The authors also mention three principles that had particular significance for the development of the F Scale. The first was that an item chosen should have the maximum of indirectness. The second was that each item should have some balance between irrationality and "objective truth;" it should neither be so "wild" that hardly anyone would agree with it nor so correct that nearly everyone would agree with it. Third, each item had to "contribute to the structural unity of the scale as a whole."

The respondents indicated whether they agreed or disagreed with each item, and also to what degree, on a scale of three. When the first version of the F Scale (made up of 38 items) was administered, the mean reliability (.74) was not bad, but was "well below what is required of a truly accurate instrument." On an item analysis, some items turned out especially poor statistically because they were unclear or ambiguous, some were so "true" that nearly everyone agreed with them, and some were

---

[18]*Ibid.,* pp. 228-241.

so "crude or openly aggressive" that nearly everyone tended to disagree. So a revision was made to increase reliability, and a reliability of .87 resulted. But the scale still contained some items that were poor statistically and a few items that needed to be dropped because they were no longer timely. Also a shorter scale was deemed desirable. So a third version was constructed. On this final revision the average of the reliability coefficients turned out to be .90 (ranging from .81 to .97), and the authors felt they now had a scale that "meets rigorous statistical standards."

In validating the F Scale, attention was given to comparing the results to those obtained in the case studies. The responses of Larry and Mack are described in some detail. Mack was a relatively high scorer on the F Scale (above the mean on all of the nine variables except *Superstition* and *Power and "toughness"*), and this seemed in general harmony with his interview materials.

As an illustration of some of the problems encountered, however, we might note that the authors expected on the basis of Mack's interview that one of his highest scores would be on *Authoritarian submission,* but his actual score was only at the group mean. The explanation given is that the items in this variable on which he scored above the mean are those expressing authoritarian submission in its purest form, while his low scores on other items in that variable resulted from the influence of his objective-scientific values. The authors say perhaps "Mack's submissive tendencies are insufficiently sublimated to permit their expression in abstract religious terms." They also note that one item which he disagreed with was an item they expected him to accept, and suggest that for some "truly submissive subjects" an item can come "too close to home," and that those subjects therefore respond contrary to their strongest feeling.

Larry scored lower than the group mean on all variables except *Authoritarian aggression.* In general, there was harmony between his responses on the F Scale and his interview materials, although there were also some surprises. For example, there was nothing in the interview material to suggest that Larry was superstitious, and yet he did agree with the astrology item. The authors suggest that perhaps "it should not be surprising to find an element of mysticism in this weak and rather passive character."[19]

G. COMMENTARY ON THE AUTHORITARIAN PERSONALITY

The Authoritarian Personality is nearly 1000 pages long and contains an enormous amount of material not even faintly alluded to here. And although there are repeated references to the measurement of "opinions, attitudes, and values," the scales constructed do not pretend to measure values in general or even a broad range of values (in addition to the F Scale, scales were developed for Anti-Semitism, Ethnocentrism, and Politico-Economic Conservatism). Even so, the book does illustrate some of the difficulties and problems likely to be encountered whenever one attempts to combine depth psychology with scale construction to measure something in the value realm.

Among the major questions arising in such an approach, in my opinion, are the following:

(1) Are there actually widespread behavior patterns of the type assumed when potential fascistic personalities are discussed? I am not here saying the answer is "no," but raising the question of what typologies are most useful, since so many different typologies can be imagined and in fact have been offered. The spatio-temporal setting of the studies in this volume helps to explain the emphasis on fascistic personalities, but perhaps in a different time and place that emphasis would seem misdirected.

(2) Clearly the authors have great confidence in various depth psychology theories, clinical interviews, the TAT, etc. Without going into the enormous literature critical of such tendencies, I will only note here a marked willingness on the part of some clinicians to rely on a kind of "fittingness" or "falling into place" of the various materials they deal with. They seem to show a penchant for developing "likely stories" that may have little or no scientific support, and often a kind of intuition is

---

[19]The materials on validation are on pp. 269 ff.; those on reliability are on pp. 242 ff.

uncritically relied upon. Whatever the merits of psychoanalyt-
ically oriented theories, various projective tests, etc., it seems
clear that many aspects of those materials have not as yet been
scientifically warranted. In any event, the heavy reliance on
them by the authors in assessing the validity of the F Scale
obviously poses the question of the validity of the clinical instruments.

(3) *The Authoritarian Personality* was a mammoth under-
taking, and some questions arise about the worth of the findings
compared to the amount of effort that went into the project.
Even if the various scales developed turn out to have less significance than was thought when the study first appeared, the
overall project still might have merit as a guide to how similar
inquiries could be improved in the future. But how to assess
the merits of the output of the investigation is not an easy matter, in view of the controversies about almost all of its major
aspects. In my opinion, in projects such as *The Authoritarian
Personality* a disproportionate amount of effort goes into the
elaboration of hypotheses and their modification on the basis
of soft evidence, and it probably would be more profitable to
concentrate attention on the confirmation of the guiding hypotheses right from the beginning.

Despite the negative tone of much that has been said, I see
no reason to doubt that a cluster of opinions and attitudes about
"antidemocratic" phenomena is found in some behavior and that
this cluster has been measured to some degree by the use of
the F Scale. I also think that the whole project indirectly indicates how relatively superficial many other studies of value are
and how willing some inquirers are to take the most "surface"
responses as indicative of values.

H. CARTER'S USE OF THE KOLOMAN TECHNIQUE

A variety of criticisms have been made of the use of questionnaires and related public opinion polling techniques. For
example, Leo Bogart argues that often the process by which a

group arrives at a position is not appropriately investigated by approaching these people separately, and says that opinion polls "generally fail to embody the rich context of motivation and cross-communication out of which opinions arise and activate people in the mass." The "confrontation" of the interviewer and the respondent may tend to force a "crystallization and expression" of opinions when there "were no more than chaotic swirls of thought." Often the procedure "forces expression into predetermined channels, by presenting clear-cut and mutually exclusive choices."

Bogart also emphasizes that he is not suggesting (as is sometimes done) that on a given subject individuals have one public opinion and one private opinion which may or may not be the same. He says:

"I am rather suggesting that one may at the same time hold a *variety* of opinions, articulated or vague, public shading into private. These multiple opinions, which correspond to different roles or reference groups, may be contradictory or incongruent . . . Just as the same object may arouse alternating emotions of love and hate, depending on circumstances, so we are capable of simultaneously incorporating a belief and its opposite or seeing the best and worst in two alternative courses of action."[20]

In an attempt to overcome some of the difficulties just mentioned, Carter developed the Koloman procedure to study certain "social values" that were involved in the composition of material to be distributed overseas.[21] Carter's research was sponsored by the U. S. Information Agency to see if information materials distributed overseas might contain assumptions about the desirability of certain things that are negatively valued in the country to which the materials are sent, to see if there are positive values in the other country that could be used in USIA appeals, etc. The subjects were Filipino and Indian nationals attending col-

[20]Leo Bogart, "No Opinion, Don't Know, and Maybe No Answer," *The Public Opinion Quarterly,* Vol. XXXI, 1967. The long quotation is from p. 342.

[21]Roy E. Carter, Jr., "An Experiment in Value Measurement," *American Sociological Review,* Vol. 21, 1956. (For another use of a Koloman-like procedure, see Ch. V, where Otto von Mering's research is described in some detail.)

lege in the San Francisco Bay Area, plus a control group of U. S. students. To help get answers to such questions, Carter wanted to find out what "is believed in, approved, or valued by the potential readers," and he developed a procedure to measure the "relative importance and/or acceptability of certain value concepts." He took 'value' as referring to the objects, qualities or conditions that satisfy motivation; i.e., as the "obverse of motives."

To help get more spontaneous and perhaps more candid responses than might be obtained through the use of questionnaires, and to save the respondents from the possible embarrassment of saying they did not have an opinion or did not wish to answer, the Koloman procedure was used. Koloman is a mythical new country (in some ways perhaps analogous to the new republics of the Philippines and India). A dialogue among a group of "explorers" in which Koloman's national goals and priorities were discussed was prepared. Each paragraph was intended to deal with a single value. The subjects, after reading the dialogue, were asked to place a single or double plus mark, or a single or double minus mark, beside each paragraph to indicate whether they agreed or disagreed, and also the intensity of their agreement or disagreement. They were not required to make any mark if they did not wish to.

The prepared dialogues discussed the type of educational system, government, birth control, race relations, religion, etc., that Koloman should have. A sample dialogue was:

> "No matter how our economy is controlled, I think we need
> to bear in mind the fact that even a country as richly endowed
> by nature as Koloman will not be prosperous for very long unless
> its population is kept within bounds. We need widespread edu-
> cation in birth control and family planning so that we will not
> be overpopulated."[22]

Carter was more interested in developing a useful approach than in trying to find "definitive" answers, and he does not make great claims for his findings. He does suggest, however, that a device of the kind he used "might prove to be a fairly painless

---

[22]*Ibid.*, p. 157.

instrument" for investigating culturally different beliefs about social values. Since the overall purpose was to develop effective information materials for a target group of influential people, the fact that the method used presupposes a literate group of subjects with a background and interest in social, political, and economic issues poses no problem.

Carter also suggests that some of the response patterns seem to indicate a "face" validation for his procedure. Thus the Filipinos (who were predominantly Catholic) were the only group responding negatively to the statement favoring birth control and were also the only group favoring writing a strong moral code into law. The Americans strongly disapproved of mass media censorship, the Indians disapproved slightly, and the Filipinos approved slightly. This fits in with what would be expected, according to Carter. And the Indians' responses "were consonant" with the impressions cited in the literature about the relatively young, westernized elite of contemporary India.

In short, Carter believes he has developed a promising technique that may be more useful than regular questionnaires for measuring the "expressed beliefs" of the subjects on certain social values. In discussing the question of the relation of public attitudes and private attitudes, he is content to cite George Lundberg's remark that the public verbal professions of influential people can have far greater social significance than the fact that those people may not live up to their professions.[23]

I. COMMENTARY ON CARTER

Carter is relatively modest about his achievements (a trait not always encountered in those who claim to have measured values), and I see no reason to doubt that he has developed a useful way of ascertaining the "expressed beliefs" of literate people interested in the issues involved in his study, or that the kind of findings he obtained could be used in developing materials for certain groups in other countries.

---

[23]George A. Lundberg, "Human Values—A Research Program," *Research Studies,* State College of Washington, Vol. 18, 1950, p. 107.

Carter also is clearer than some writers about the restrictions on the range of his findings. For example, he emphasizes that there may be subtle semantic differences among groups of subjects, even those who have a fair grasp of English. But since his sample was screened to eliminate those whose English language proficiency seemed deficient, and since presumably the ultimate readers of the materials would have a good grasp of English, he had no great concern over that issue.

In general, for a project of the type he had in mind, his procedures seem reasonable and appropriate. The extent to which values are equivalent to the types of belief Carter studied is another matter, and possibly a more accurate title for his paper could be found. Many of the issues mentioned earlier occur here also, such as the relation of attitudes, motives, etc., to values, and the wisdom of taking verbal responses as central in value inquiry. Since those issues have already been commented on, they will not be discussed again in relation to Carter's specific research.

J.   CONCLUSION

In this chapter, we have noted a variety of social and psychological attempts to measure values. The investigations discussed were chosen as representative of the work done in this area, not as either the best or worst that could be found. We have considered the use of simple rank-order techniques, of relatively straightforward questionnaires, and attempts to overcome some presumed difficulties in those techniques. We have discussed inquiries based on the notion that values can be gotten at through relatively "surface" manifestations, and a study that emphasized "depth" factors instead.

As mentioned throughout the chapter, some of the least satisfactory aspects of such work concern validity. One reason is that there is so little clarity as to what 'value' is taken as. In the materials surveyed in this chapter, for example, there is oscillation between locating a value within the person (i.e., his motives, needs, desires, etc.) and within the environment (i.e., what would satisfy a motive, a need, etc.) We have noted tension between construing values as desires and construing them as what a person or group views as desir*able*. Surely discussions of validity are likely to be highly defective until greater clarity is achieved about such matters.

In a general way, I see no reason to doubt that all the studies mentioned do measure (crudely) some behavior that is elicited in a given set of circumstances. Although all the studies claim that value behavior was measured, clearly several different types of behavior were investigated. The overall terminological confusion is immense, and this permits considerable uncertainty both about what is being measured and its significance for human affairs.

For a complete study of human behavior, private and public expressions of preferences, desires, beliefs, attitudes, etc., can be useful, as well as both "surface" and "depth" manifestations of those types of behavior. It may be useful to find out how people say they will respond in a given setting, and how they in fact do respond in that setting. We need clarity as to what is being measured and how. The problem is not that so many different things are involved in alleged measures of values, but that they become confused either in the inquiry itself, or in the dissemination of the results, or both.

Chapter V

A GRAMMAR OF HUMAN VALUES

A. INTRODUCTION

Otto von Mering is an anthropologist who has strong psychological and philosophical interests. Unlike some behavioral scientists writing on values, he has commented extensively on the general methodological considerations he sees as relevant to the investigation of values. His book[1] goes far beyond what is usually contained in an anthropological field report or what is typically discussed when sociologists, social psychologists, and psychologists attempt to measure values.

Von Mering's book has five interrelated objectives. He developed a "general theory of human valuation . . . which integrates a wide range of thought from the behavioral sciences and philosophy." This theory was used in behavioral research to help develop a "grammar of common, possible human values." In order to use that classificatory system, he invented an instrument for obtaining "comparable and quantifiable data on moral codes and ethical ideas in two or more cultures." Data were gathered on two Southwestern U. S. subcultures (Texas homesteaders and a Mormon village) to show that a "reliable and systematic analysis of the patterning of values" can be made for those two groups. Finally, his work shows that the "degree of social contact between

---

[1] Otto von Mering, *A Grammar of Human Values*, Pittsburgh, University of Pittsburgh Press, 1961.

members of different cultures" is related to the cultural and individual profiles of valuing.[2]

In this chapter more emphasis will be put on the general methodological issues raised by von Mering than on the specific results of his inquiry into the values of the Texas homesteaders and the Mormons. That is done not because his specific results are unimportant or uninteresting, but because so many behavioral science investigations of values ignore or minimize the general context of inquiry in which such work is carried on. His book raises a good number of the fundamental problems to be faced by any alleged scientific treatment of values.

B.   VON MERING'S BASIC POINT OF VIEW

Von Mering begins Chapter I by saying that although sociologists and anthropologists have been keenly interested in taboos, they often show little awareness of a particular taboo affecting their own work—the assumption that there is some absolute difference between *value* and *fact* and that values cannot be appropriately studied in a scientific manner. Von Mering argues both that the values of the scientist often affect his scientific work and that it is scientifically feasible to investigate individual and group values.[3]

In developing his theory of value and an appropriate methodology for describing the value patterns of the two subcultures, von Mering relied on certain guiding principles. One such principle involves what is often called a *biosocial* approach:

"Our basic premise is that knowing and valuing are social facts, and, therefore, analyzable within a scheme of social action. Their origins are traceable to the social as well as biological nature of man. We know that man in any culture has a persistent urge for developing and abiding by systems of valuation to answer the problem of the meaning of his existence. We also know that, although the specific expressions of these systems

[2] *Ibid.*, pp. ix-x.
[3] *Ibid.*, pp. 3-6.

vary from culture to culture, and within limits from individual to individual, there exist inevitables of *human* existence in which these expressions have their root."[4]

He also assumes that valuation occurs primarily (but not exclusively) when something should be eliminated, when conflicts have to be resolved, or when there is a lack, privation, or need. He does *not* assume that all valuation presupposes conflict or tension, and points out that valuing itself may produce tension or conflict. This general approach links his work to some of the themes encountered in American naturalistic philosophers such as John Dewey, R. B. Perry, and S. C. Pepper. Although he does not make much use of the transactional framework proposed by Dewey and A. F. Bentley, there is at least a family resemblance to that framework in many of von Mering's views.

In discussing the relation of empirical data to theory construction, von Mering says that three types of methodological principle have been used to analyze social science data: the historical-descriptive, the systematic-deductive, and the empirical-deductive. The first arranges data "in a longitudinal and cross-sectional fashion." The second is the characteristic method of theoretical mathematics. Von Mering prefers the third method:

"The empirical deductive method of theory construction is patterned after the canons of mathematical physics. The social scientist using this method is not satisfied with generating *a priori* structures or hypothetical categories that fit logically. Rather, he tries to construct theory in such a way that the generalizations are both deductively interrelated and phrased as variables that are empirically measurable and verifiable. In doing so he must, however, guard against making his theory too narrowly selective and being content with merely establishing empirically already existing ideas."

In discussing the relation of "theoretical constructs" to "reality," von Mering says:

---

[4]*Ibid.,* p. 13. See also pp. 68-69.

"So long as the researcher is content to conceive of all scientific knowledge as *probable,* and as *organizing* experience, though not descriptive of its ultimate real nature, and as *systematic* but acceptant of alternative systems, and finally, as *contextual,* that is, objective but relative to a public frame of reference, he need not hesitate to proceed."[5]

In general, von Mering's theoretical orientation was influenced by the logical positivists and the pragmatists among philosophers, and by such social scientists as Durkheim, Mannheim, Weber, Parsons, and Kluckhohn. As the quotations just cited suggest, although von Mering takes mathematical physics as a model, as did some of the positivists, he moves somewhat in the direction of the transactionalism of Dewey and Bentley. But he also puts more emphasis on the "subjective" than do many other writers, which may be partly due to the influence of some of the social scientists just mentioned. To illustrate, in a brief discussion of *need,* he says:

"A need is here not viewed merely as a biological or environmental pressure. The individual primarily perceives and experiences the existence of needs and wishes to act upon them when he has made a declaration or assertion of needs. No more is necessary for the individual than to sense the 'in-and of itself' of a need."[6]

If I understand that passage correctly, he puts strong emphasis on the "subjective" sensing of a need and less emphasis on the "objective" set of circumstances that presumably gave rise to the need.

I raise such matters at this time, not to criticize von Mering particularly, but to illustrate the complexity of value inquiry, including the unsettled state of the terminology used. We are so far from having firm names for the various phases and aspects of the transactional fields we are trying to investigate that often communication is extremely difficult.

---

[5]*Ibid.* The first quotation is from pp. 51-52; the second is from p. 66.
[6]*Ibid.,* p. 69, note 23.

C. RESEARCH DESIGN

As noted, von Mering wanted to analyze the patterns of valuational behavior of two small subcultures, and he sees valuing as a "social fact." In his view, man is not simply a reacting organism, but has interpretive and expressive capacities. In solving various problems and dilemmas characteristic of human life, men have developed a variety of valuational systems. Both on the individual and the group levels, human life develops tensions, dilemmas, and paradoxes. A valuational system useful in one context may have to change as the context changes. One way a person finds of adjusting to others is through his value patterns:

> "Just as systems of valuation are at the core of a culture's means for tackling these paradoxes, so it is for the individual in relating himself to his society. This relatedness is dominantly patterned after his culture through a normal process of assimilation or internalization of values. On the other hand, the content of his value pattern is changeable. A person's experiences of socialization are variable, both in early life and as an adult; and he may also acquire special new insights in the course of contacts with people of a different background. The nature of these experiences tends to determine whether the basis of his valuations broaden or become narrowed. In some respects, his basic value system will be unique for him alone, but he may share much of it with an inner circle of friends. It may also deviate radically from the cultural system of values, or it may lie within the permissible range encompassed by the cultural system."[7]

Von Mering saw the American Southwest as offering many examples of what is involved in such matters. Five cultural groups (Zuni, Navaho, Spanish-American, Mormon, and Texan) co-existed in the same ecological area and had been in continuous face-to-face relation for at least one generation. His research dealt with Rimrock villagers, who were Mormon irrigation farmers and cattlemen, and Homestead villagers, who were Texan dry land bean farmers. He focused on the attitudes of those two groups to the Navahos.

---

[7] *Ibid.,* p. 14.

In the early stages of the study, von Mering decided that "standard interview, questionnaire, or scaling procedures were inadequate for a systematic analysis of valuation and value patterns." He devised a new procedure called the *Theme-Controlled Discussion Technique (TCDT)*. This has some resemblance to the Koloman technique discussed in Chapter IV, Section H, and stems in part from earlier work done in sociological and psychotherapeutic group discussion contexts. The *TCDT* was designed to reduce the interviewer's stimulation of responses to a minimum and to favor maximum responsiveness of group discussants to each other. Von Mering notes that in such situations people respond differently than if they were interviewed alone. It is likely, for example, that in the group setting a person will not voice views that he would be inclined to consider only in principle or for the sake of argument. On the other hand, von Mering believes that the group approach "is apt to be more sensitive to the possible range of overtly expressed and operationally sanctioned ideal and practical values" than is the individual interview approach.

The groups selected each contained three members, and were assembled with an eye to their mutual friendliness and to their availability for the scheduled meetings. The discussions were recorded by an unobtrusive microphone, the existence of which was mentioned to the participants. Each discussion group was presented with an invariant verbal stimulus consisting of a recorded dialogue structured around a specific and difficult social problem familiar to all the discussants. The stimulus conversation presented a variety of conflicting values. A method of codifying and comparing reactions was also developed.[8]

Von Mering also describes briefly the field work conditions. He had to be accepted in three roles: as a researcher, as a participant observer, and as a person with his own habits and personality. How this acceptance is achieved depends, of course, on the type of culture one is studying. For example, von Mering was able to quote from one of the Mormon apostles that authority must bow before experimental methods, and in setting up the

---

[8]*Ibid.*, pp. 24-28.

discussion groups he made frequent reference to the Mormon gospel statement that three people constitute a perfect group. Much of this information about gaining acceptance is fascinating and helps to show the intricate set of circumstances that may be involved in data gathering.

Von Mering says it is desirable to begin the task of devising a systematic scheme for value analysis by adopting an attitude of "beneficent scepticism" toward the data. As he read through the remarks made in the discussion groups, he wrote down whatever "potentially invariant points of reference—individual value items, attitudes, or defense mechanisms—he could conceivably apply to the data." A few samples follow:

1) A respondent said: "I guess that the Navaho tribe is the worst rundown tribe there is, isn't it? Is the ignorantest tribe there is." Van Mering's comments on this are: "Evidence of rigidity; education or knowledge viewed as an absolute standard of individual worth or deficiency; implication of a didactic condemnation of those who violate this standard."

2) A respondent said: "Well, it looks like—if they are ever going to get ahead, they'd have to own some land of their own. Don't look like they could be working for somebody else all their lives. However, I think some 'em are—well—it's more like 'em to be lazier than we are." Von Mering's comments are: "Strong concern for material possessions and independence of others as criteria for progress; a case of blame-placing, and implicit denial of personal negative traits in area of economic productivity."

3) A respondent said: "I think you need some classroom, but I think they need practical education, too. Together with the rest of us that would help 'em. I think their standards of living would be raised lots." Von Mering commented: "Humanitarian and affiliative regard for outgroup; realistic, comprehensive, and constructive suggestion for equalization of economic advantages."

4) A respondent said: "Well, self-confidence and our neighbors' confidence helped us more than the Indian. You bring an Indian down here and you know doggone well you are not going to have too much confidence in that guy and nobody else. This

is what I say, confidence—we haven't got doubts about every guy as the Navaho." Von Mering commented: "Self-satisfied stress on self-reliance and reciprocity within in-group; blaming outgroup for being distrustful of each other; distrust used for rationalizing speakers' distrust of the Navahos."[9]

Von Mering then says that such samples of attitudes and his notations show how complex it is to develop an operationally useful set of invariant reference points. However, his preliminary and impressionistic work enabled him to formulate a value theory and to develop what he saw as a logical and workable system for classifying values.

As he went over the data, he felt he could identify roughly thirty-eight (heterogeneous and sometimes overlapping) value and attitude categories. Applying those categories to the data showed that several groups of opposable values and attitudes turned up in the Rimrock and Homestead data. He then regrouped the original series of categories into two sets, each having fifteen related categories. Even so, "most of the categories still were rather global entities." The data were re-examined, and the existing categories were subdivided and again applied to the data. More changes were called for, and it now seemed possible to distinguish between attitudes and values. All the attitudinal categories were eliminated; the remaining values were reclassified and made more precise. This resulted in a total of thirty-four categories. It also turned out that some values occurred more frequently in association with other values than independently. Overall, the values fell into four groups or realms of valuing, and into two sets of opposable values. With a few minor changes (such as adding two value categories), this became the basis for his grammar of human values, and a set of scoring conventions was devised to make up the whole classificatory instrument.[10]

Before reviewing von Mering's grammar of values, which is done in Section E, it seems useful to explore in some detail his notion of value, since he refined his earlier views in the light of the work just mentioned.

---

[9]*Ibid.,* pp. 53-62. The field work conditions are described on pp. 41-47.
[10]*Ibid.,* pp. 62-64.

D.　VALUES AND VALUE EXPERIENCE

On the basis of his study of Rimrock and Homestead and of his general reflection on the topic, von Mering arrived at some notions of what values are and how they are related to experience. He argues that there is no need to assume fixed or absolute values that should be sought by all men, but also says a "metaphysical discussion of the consequences of rejecting a view of values as eternal absolutes is beyond the scope of this presentation." On the other hand, men often believe that some values "have the compelling force of universality." Indeed, according to von Mering, "we can say that the paramount value for man is life itself." In addition to that "ultimate value," men may have other values that are regarded as immutable. He also notes that impressive anthropological evidence is available indicating that different cultures have quite different criteria for distinguishing between the valuable and the nonvaluable, just as they have different criteria for differentiating between fact and nonfact.

Von Mering agrees with Dewey that merely enjoying or desiring something does not make it a value. Nor is a value to be identified with an interest, as Perry and others did. Von Mering goes on:

> "To the individual, values are *more* than just culturally held and transmitted cognitive referents or 'conceptions' for the diverse practices which form the matrix of human conduct and also relate man to the human universe. We can draw inferences from conceptions and project them into the future, but we cannot directly know from them 'how life makes itself go,' or how it will or may turn out. We say that values *as such,* i.e., as scientifically classifiable data, are other than existence. However, on the level of experience they are related to or rather, a vital aspect of human existence through the individual who *thinks, feels,* and *acts.*"[11]

Some parts of that quotation are not clear to me, such as the insistence that values as such are other than existence although

[11]References in this section are from pp. 64-71 of von Mering; the long quotation is from p. 67.

they are a vital aspect of human existence. Perhaps what von Mering wants to emphasize is the "force" values can have for the individual. He says, for example: "Values are, so to speak, 'living' entities to the experiencing individual who in the course of repetitive valuing becomes committed to them in conduct." He also notes that values do not merely "exist as referents in the individual's thought-space," but have a marked emotional significance for the individual in carrying on his activities. Emotional commitment may be an important factor in situations in which other people hold different values and a conflict then arises.

Von Mering is interested in how values are generated from human behavior and why some values, in contrast to others, become socially institutionalized. He maintains that all values "arise by asserting some claim to be socially memorable and honorable." Through time some values are established in a particular cultural setting. If a value is stabilized over a long period and is not challenged, it will probably lose its earlier plasticity and be experienced by the members of the culture as something imposed on the individual.

In a particular culture, the range of possible values from which a person can select is extensive and probably goes beyond the experience of any one individual. In some circumstances, a person is quite free to choose from those values; in other circumstances he may feel that he must passively accept what others accept. And although testing and verification of values occurs in terms of their usefulness as guides to action, we should not construe valuation as too intellectual, for "most cultural values emerge into or are present in individual consciousness without continuous re-verification by evidential facts."

Von Mering agrees with Dewey that some of the conventional sharp distinctions between means and ends are not warranted. For von Mering, "neither means nor ends have an independent existence of their own"; they rather "represent a continuum." He goes on:

"In any description and classification of the many possible individual and cultural values, it is useful to assume that the term *value,* apart from encompassing means and ends, is not restricted to the ethical or normative realm alone. The possible values an individual may hold and share with his culture tend to embrace what is *existential* and essential for human survival, both in the cultural and individual sense; what is *normative* or morally and legally descriptive, directive and regulative; and what is *idiosyncratic* or represents personal, projective judgments and pronouncements."[12]

Finally, von Mering rejects the view that certain values are always prepotent in comparison to other values: the "binding power" of a value is "a matter of individual selection and acceptance in the light of his particular life situation and life history." Values are taken as implicitly showing the direction behavior may take and as having a potential binding power on the valuer that is realized in the course of his valuations.

In his value theory, then, von Mering combines a variety of strands found in the literature. He does not offer a succinct formal account of the referent of 'value.' On the one hand, he is inclined to give considerable weight to how individuals perceive or think about values, although he certainly does not follow the path either of ordinary language philosophers or of intuitionists in ethical theory. On the other hand, he is committed to a scientific approach to values, and this leads him to be skeptical of some things individuals may subjectively feel about value phenomena. He takes one of the main functions of valuation to be a guide to action, and he emphasizes the cultural aspects of values. Yet, he also touches upon existentialist themes stressing the personal, the subjective, and the individual.

E.   GRAMMAR OF POSSIBLE VALUES

As noted, on the basis of his data von Mering found that he could group most of the values into four categories. Since our purpose is not a detailed critique of von Mering's work, but rather its general significance for value measurement, I will not

---

12*Ibid.,* p. 70.

give a full account of his grammar, but only enough to show how he proceeds.

Value Realm I he calls the SIMPLISTIC VALUE REALM. Here, von Mering places responses characteristic of those who have a low intensity of social experience and who emphasize such matters as external, hedonistic, and private standards. Von Mering puts nine value clusters in this realm, two of which will be mentioned to illustrate what is involved. Code S1 (using the code symbols will be useful later on) designates the cluster he calls *General substantive, conventional, and moralistic values.* Statements exemplifying this value cluster express "a vague sense of virtue and purity or 'pure thoughts'." Duty, integrity, standards, morality, etc., are emphasized. Code S5 designates the cluster called *Hedonism and "selfish human nature,"* and statements made in this category express a view of man as basically selfish, self-indulging, and motivated by greed.

In contrast and opposed to the Simplistic Value Realm is von Mering's group IV, the COMPREHENSIVE VALUE REALM. Here are found the expressions characteristic of people having intensive and extensive social experience; such people often put much emphasis on universal or holistic values in the solution of problems. The standards preferred tend to encompass and sometimes transcend the particular life situations of all or most people. Realms I and IV are believed by von Mering to lie at the opposite ends of a continuum. He refers to the Weberian-Parsonian notion of particularism and universalism; his two value realms constitute a modification of that approach.

Realm IV has eight clusters, three of which will be mentioned for illustrative purposes. C2 is the label for *Liberal and humanistic codes.* Here we find responses that emphasize such notions as equality of opportunity, equal chance, a "fair shake," etc. C3 is the label for *Comprehensive—constructive assessment of education, knowledge, and progress.* The emphasis is on the perfectibility of man and society through education and knowledge. C7 is called *Relational and wholistic interpretations of conduct,* and involves a belief that means and ends are part of an interdependent whole and an emphasis on the interconnections of the various aspects of a whole.

Von Mering argues that there are two additional value realms worth differentiating, which are "logically and experientially" closely related to the two just discussed. In the two additional realms, emphasis is placed on various specific aspects of personal and interpersonal aspects of living, while in I and IV the values are less specific and more theoretical.

Realm II is called the ISOLATIVE PERSONAL VALUE REALM, and includes interpersonal values that have a socially inclusive, but yet situation-bound, emphasis. This realm is closest to I, but its range of application to practical life problems is not as limited or confining. On the other hand, it is not as inclusive as Realm IV. Primary emphasis is on "group-ethics" of the type that compartmentalizes human experience into authoritarian and utilitarian areas. Two of the ten subdivisions in Realm II will be mentioned. Sis 3 designates the cluster called *Male traits and self-preservation,* and is used when "he-man" or "tough guy" traits are mentioned. Sis 8 is the code symbol for *Sacred religions and secular dogma.* Subjects scoring heavily in this area tend to view all human conduct from a particular ideological perspective, religious or political.

The last realm to be discussed (III) is called the INCLUSIVE INTERPERSONAL VALUE REALM. The values located here, says von Mering, are more logically inclusive, and experientially more appropriate and adaptive, than those located in the isolative-personal realm. The values in Realm III are closely related to the comprehensive values of Realm IV, and at least theoretically are applicable to all aspects of interpersonal life.

There are nine sets of values within Realm III, two of which will be mentioned for illustrative purposes. Cin 1 is called *Relational authority, mutuality and nurture.* Here statements made by the subjects emphasize the importance of mutuality, situational support, etc., in all human relations, business and social. Cin 7 designates *Interest identity and cooperative competition.* In this category, certain types of competition and conflicts are regarded as helpful and desirable in terms of furthering internal adaptation as well as biological and social survival. Such cooperative competition is distinguished from a hostile type of "struggle for survival."[13]

Lengthy protocols are given for each value cluster in each of the four value realms. As mentioned, the group discussions stimulated by a prepared dialogue were recorded, and the values contained in those discussions were coded in terms of the protocols. Three examples will help show how the inquiry proceeded.

(1) The following sentence occurred in one of the group discussions: "Well, them Navahos just need an even break; and if they had it the whites and they could compete and cooperate a lot better." Von Mering says: "This statement shows a stress on an equal chance (Code C2), on friendly competition (Code Cin 7), and it implies a wholistic or perspectival view of the means-ends relationship (Code C7)."

(2) Another response in a group discussion was: "The Lord when he put these Indians over here, they drifted into indolence and degradation, they wouldn't do a day's work. But you know, they'll be able to show their ability to grow if we whites and them get together, mixed with 'em and helped more; and they're going to do it regardless, the time's acoming, it's just as sure as the 'word'." According to von Mering: "Here we see how sacred religious dogma is invoked (Code Sis 8), and we notice a stress on inadequate economic performance (Code Sis 3), on individual potential perfectability (Code C3), on nurturance and affiliation (Code Cin 1), and the existence of an implicit perspectivism (Code C7)."

(3) The discussion statement was: "They do—want something for nothing, it's very bad." Von Mering coded that S1 and S5.[14]

Before going further, we might note that a fair amount of interpretation is involved; for example in (1) above a rather brief statement is interpreted as exemplifying three different value clusters. Also of interest is that protocols developed by highly literate, educated, and sophisticated people are being applied to statements that reflect a much lower level of education. (This is

---

[13]Material in this section is from pp. 90-180 of von Mering. An outline of the grammar of values is on pp. 96-98.

[14]*Ibid.*, pp. 257-258.

not to say there is necessarily anything wrong in such procedures, but only to point to possible misunderstandings whenever the inquirer is from a much different sociocultural milieu than the person whose oral responses he is coding.)

In his section on validation and reliability, von Mering reminds us of the setting of his study. He developed a grammar of values that can be regarded as:

> ". . . a treatise on the classes of possible values that exist in any contemporary society of the Western World. It provides us with a structural arrangement of value forms that shows how distinctions in the apperception of reality are marked, and what are the mutual relations, uses, and functions of values in the course of their expression."[15]

He took as an operating assumption that the values selected by a person in assessing human problems mirror cultural value patterns. Also, both cultural and individual value patterns presume a process of selective internalization or assimilation of particular values from the total grammar of possible values. It was hoped, then, that the grammar of values would provide "a general, systematic and comprehensive framework to obtain a series of standard indices about the patterning of human valuation."

As he points out, the construction of this type of system is a relatively new type of endeavor, and many questions can be raised about its validity (does the instrument measure what we want or think it is measuring?). One possible criticism of his grammar is that it is too "neat and tidy." Von Mering argues that since he takes the valuation process as mainly a "trending" in the direction of one or another value cluster, his instrument is not inflexible. He also says that when he applied his instrument to the broad issue of Navaho-white adjustment, he found it useful and gained many insights.

He further argues that if the categories in his grammar were admitted to be reasonably adequate representations of what is found in valuing behavior, the whole instrument could be said to have a kind of "prima facie" or "intrinsic" validity. One way of getting at that issue would be to ask a group of experts to

---

[15]*Ibid.*, p. 180.

evaluate each of the categories in the grammar. Von Mering did so. He prepared some cards containing brief accounts of each of the thirty-six categories, gave other instructions, and asked six experienced behavioral scientists to rate each of the categories. Each judge was requested to indicate which of the categories a universalistic valuer (as contrasted to a particularistic valuer) would most accept and which he would most object to, when confronted with a delicate social issue. There was marked agreement among the judges, although some doubts were expressed. In general, the judges agreed that the items in the grammar of values did represent "an ordered sample of possible values which people could use regularly according to the degree of their universalistic or particularistic orientation."[16]

Von Mering argues that the construction of standard indices of human valuation rests on the notion that there is "some kind of unity or pattern" in the type of data he is dealing with. The task is to set up "reference points" and so relate them that the patterning is revealed. He continues:

> "As we have seen, these reference points have to do with types of possible goals and means, and methods of decision favored in a given society. They also deal with sets of sanctioned and denied forms of conduct, approved and disfavored character traits, and other kinds of concepts and controls that have validity or moral status in a given culture. The grammar of values as a whole is deemed inclusive insofar as it permits the classification of nearly every verbal act into at least one of the constituent value categories."[17]

Finally, he also discusses the range of application of his instrument. He mentions that no validation has been attempted for its application to all relevant human contexts, although it might well prove useful for other cultures than those investigated. On the other hand, he emphasizes that his categories are culture-bound in the sense that they reflect Western values in general, and two subcultures in particular, more than values prevailing in other parts of the world.

---

[16]*Ibid.*, p. 184.
[17]*Ibid.*, p. 185.

Von Mering also discusses the reliability of his instrument, or the degree to which repeated uses of the instrument on the same data will produce the same results. He personally scored the data. He then, as a check on reliability, used two other coders. One of the coders was a physical anthropologist with extensive experience in anthropometry; the other a psychologist with much experience in psychometrics. Both were trained for one week and thereafter coded some material (protocols of one Rimrock and one Homestead discussion group) independently of each other. The anthropologist had a 95.7% agreement with von Mering, and the psychologist a 92.0% agreement. The agreements were based on "gross" rather than "net" reliability; i.e., no test was made of the inter-rater agreement on each category for each of the subjects, but only of the composite rating for all the categories. The high rate of agreement found leads von Mering to say that the use of his instrument can "nearly reach objectivity."[18]

F.   SOME RESULTS

The analysis of the protocols produced a total of 2,745 value scores for Homestead and 2,352 for Rimrock. Using approximate figures, 35% of all the valuing of the Homesteaders, and 26% of the valuing of the Rimrockers, occurred in the Simplistic Value Realm (I). For the Isolative Value Realm (II), the totals were 26% for Homestead and 25% for Rimrock. For the Inclusive Interpersonal Value Realm (III), Homesteaders totalled 17% and Rimrockers 21%. For the Comprehensive Value Realm (IV), the totals were 22% for Homestead and 28% for Rimrock.

A comparative value profile was made, in which Realms II and III were assigned to the horizontal axis, and Realms I and IV to the vertical axis. Where the axes intersect was made equal to zero, and the distance marked off on each axis from the zero point indicated the percentage standing of each subculture in each Realm. It was apparent that the profiles for the two subcultures diverged markedly along the vertical axis, but not along the horizontal. Von Mering continues:

[18]*Ibid.*, pp. 186-189.

"They are at opposite poles in their use of simplistic and comprehensive values, but similarly oriented to the isolative personal value realm which focuses on desirable situation-bound, in-group patterns of conduct. Both communities appear to be less strongly committed to inclusive interpersonal values than to the other value realms. The uniqueness of these value profiles is not a matter of chance. A series of tests of significance which have been applied to the percentage standings of each culture in the four value realms bear this out."[19]

When the tests were made, it was found that the profiles for Homestead and Rimrock differed significantly in Realms I and IV. Although there were differences in respect to Realm III, they were not significant statistically. Performances in Realm II were statistically identical. In general, Rimrock had more universalistic values and Homestead had more particularistic values.

Von Mering believes that some of his results have considerable theoretical interest, since the assumption was often made in the literature that the Rimrock group, because of its historical background, would emphasize community cooperation and the oneness of community and church strongly, and would not value competition, independence, self-orientation, etc., as much as would the Homesteaders. But von Mering's results indicate that both groups were about equal in their preference for individualistic and rational utilitarian values; both showed about the same lack of preference for the inclusive interpersonal values.

Value profiles were also constructed for many individuals. Von Mering argues that in every culture there will be some deviance of the individual's profile from that of the culture as a whole. For his sample, the range of agreement varied from the small to the nearly complete; uniquely variant value profiles occurred in both subcultures, but there were also people who came close to reproducing the cultural profile. He discusses the general community reaction to those who deviate considerably from the cultural norms and relates his work to other work in that area. Worth noting is that individuals whose profiles were nearly carbon-copies of their cultures did not seem to be particularly

---

[19]*Ibid.*, pp. 193-194.

content, did not necessarily have a high degree of social acceptance or prominence in the community, and were not unusually
successful economically. Also, some of the deviants from the
cultural norms were highly respected and accepted.

Von Mering discusses at length some of the cultural factors
that may account for the value profiles, relates his inquiry to
those of other workers, and in general gives extensive detail not
mentioned here.[20]

G. COMMENTARY

From my point of view, von Mering's book has two main
virtues: he discusses more fully the various assumptions he makes
(philosophical, psychological, and anthropological) than do many
other behavioral scientists writing on values, and his work illustrates in some depth the type of problem many current behavioral
investigations of value encounter.

Quite often, writers who claim to have measured values start
almost immediately with a description of the instrument they use,
and devote most of their discussion to an account of the statistical
treatment of their results or other technical "internal" matters.
Von Mering has the great merit of discussing his view of scientific
method, the network of assumptions he makes about valuation
processes, the problems of anthropological fieldwork, etc.

As is typical of much recent behavioral work on values, von
Mering takes as his basic data certain verbal responses. Without
at the moment raising any questions about that, let us note some
of the problems that are raised by his inquiry.

(1) As already noted, controversies abound as to what
scientific inquiry is and what techniques are appropriate for given
areas of investigation. Although von Mering has some sympathy
for what is sometimes called the "hard-science" approach, he also
is sympathetic to some "softer" techniques. Without exploring
those issues further, I want merely to mention that the actual
research conducted may be affected in a significant way by what
is regarded as scientifically appropriate.

---

[20]*Ibid.*, pp. 227-239.

(2)   Obviously enough, anthropological field work always poses some potential difficulties about the adequacy of the grasp of the inquirer of a different cultural setting. Human misunderstandings of others even in the same cultural group are hardly rare occurrences, and the risk may be even greater in dealing with members of a different culture. This is not at all to imply that either anthropologists in general or von Mering in particular are uncritical about such matters, but only to indicate that a cross-cultural study of values may encounter some special difficulties.

(3)   Once it is assumed that the relevant data will consist of verbal responses, a host of problems arise about what type of responses will be collected and under what circumstances. Conventional questionnaires have their own problems. Von Mering rejected their use in his inquiry, on the grounds that more adequate results would be obtained through the use of *TCDT* techniques. Any such decision opens, at least in principle, a host of questions about the relative adequacy of different techniques; for example, the influence of other members of the discussion group on the responses of a member of that group. Von Mering discusses such problems, but again different investigators might arrive at different conclusions.

(4)   Once having settled on a technique for obtaining responses, von Mering was faced with the problem of devising a suitable instrument for measuring those responses. He is candid and thorough in discussing the process by which he arrived at his value clusters, and it is praiseworthy that his basic approach was to study the data to see what categories seemed most appropriate. But it is also clear that a great deal of interpretation had already gone into the materials; as mentioned, in the first instance von Mering read a sample statement and then tried to note all possible values involved in it. How adequate his interpretation was of the intentions of the respondents is an interesting question. Even if other trained coders respond about as von Mering did, there still is some question as to whether the commonality of the coders' decisions might not be as attributable to their similar training, background, etc., as to what was intended by the re-

spondents. There are also the questions of validation and reliability that von Mering raised.

(5)   Once the results are coded, further statistical treatment
was made. Without suggesting that there was anything wrong in
von Mering's work, there can be disagreements among experts in
that area.

In short, and to belabor the obvious, in comparison with
some other areas of measurement, the measures of value arrived
at by von Mering pose a large number of problems, technical
and methodological. On numerous occasions von Mering makes
it clear that he is fully aware of the complexity of what he is
doing, so my remarks should not be taken as criticism of him for
overlooking possible difficulties. My point is rather that an
overall assessment of the worth of his inquiry would involve a
great many decisions in a variety of areas. The overall complexity,
uncertainty, and controversial aspects of von Mering's type of
approach may make a concerted effort along some other line desirable.

This, then brings me to my two main negative criticisms of
von Mering. First, I find no clear specification of what 'value'
designates. I certainly find it admirable that von Mering did not
begin with some *a priori* notion of what a value is, and he tells
us how his views became clearer only after he had been immersed
in his materials for a considerable length of time. And indeed,
he gives us numerous clues as to his use of 'value.' But in view
of the many conflicting uses of that term in the literature, and
the differing kinds of behavior to which the various uses refer,
it is extremely difficult to assess the adequacy of any particular
instrument unless we are clearly informed as to what it is supposed to measure. On certain views of what 'value' designates,
von Mering's instrument may be grossly defective; on some other
view it might be admirable.

Second, I suspect that using verbal responses as the best
indication of what value is involved may be mistaken. Again,
this is a question that can hardly be discussed intelligently unless
one first knows what he is talking about when he uses 'value.'
What I am stressing is not the need for some logically neat and

tidy formulation, but simply that the inspection of a given statement may not at all tell us which of many possibilities is intended by the person who made the statement.

To take an old example, suppose someone says: "Apples are good." Perhaps we can all agree that for a normal hungry man, eating an apple is somehow a value situation. But is the value the apple itself, the eating of it, the satiation or quiescence of hunger, some combination of those, or something else? Whatever the speaker had in mind when he said "Apples are good" is not clear simply on inspection of that statement. Further, in many alleged value situations it may be vital to distinguish between the *desired* and the *desirable,* since a person may have a strong desire for something (e.g., smoking cigarettes) but he also may find that behavior undesirable.

As discussed in Chapter III of the present book, there are important and potentially confusing issues about the relation between verbal responses and other behavior. For example, one of von Mering's respondents said about Navahos going to integrated schools: "Ten to one I would rather have them than the colored person in my school. A hundred to one."[21] How such an expression of opinion would relate to his behavior as a citizen in relation to instituting integrated schools is a matter that cannot be ascertained simply by an investigation of his response in a *TCDT* situation, although perhaps some useful hints could be gained.

Putting this another way, once we know that a certain proportion of Rimrock responses fall into one of von Mering's categories, I suspect that might indeed by a useful predictor of how other Rimrockers would verbally respond in similar situations. But what is the relation of a person's response to a stimulus dialogue to other forms of his behavior? Or, what is the warrant for the heavy stress that *values* are being measured in von Mering's work? Choice, decision, preference, approval, etc., are so characteristic of much human behavior that if we are to talk about values we need to know just which aspects of human behavior are being discussed.

---

[21] *Ibid.,* p. 259.

Related to the foregoing point and to measurement in general, it seems apparent that von Mering's measurements are relatively crude (although they certainly could be useful even so). One aspect of measurement often mentioned is the intensity or "strength" of a value (see Chapter VII of this book, for example). Von Mering takes this into account to some extent when he says that the more often a person responds to a given stimulus with a value statement, the more weight he attaches to that value. In order to have some measure of this, von Mering adopted the following convention:

> ". . . we found it useful that the analyst adopt an arbitrary line-space convention. A value code is entered only once for a given statement that does not exceed five typed lines, each line containing approximately fourteen words. A tally is entered again if the same value reoccurs in the next five lines of the statement."[22]

This, it seems to me, is quite a crude measure, and makes the assumption of a regular relation between the "weight" a person attaches to a given value and the number of times he mentions it in a particular setting. As discussed in the chapter dealing with Hull, would not an attempt to measure valuating behavior more directly offer greater promise? I suspect that important correlations can be found between the responses elicited on the *TCDT* and other forms of the respondent's behavior, and in any event verbal responses often may be a good starting point. My remarks are directed toward the importance of which aspects of the processes involved are construed as values.

Despite my criticisms, I want to reaffirm my admiration for the thoroughness of von Mering's work and the merit it has for revealing clearly some of the many difficulties of measuring values.[23]

---

[22]*Ibid.*, p. 257.

[23]Prof. von Mering kindly read an earlier version of this chapter. His comments helped improve significantly the accuracy of my summary of his research. I am grateful for his gracious aid.

Chapter VI

UTILITY, RATIONALITY, AND FORMAL APPROACHES TO VALUE

A. OVERVIEW

With the exception of the materials on measurement theory, most of the work discussed so far about the measurement of values has concerned empirical inquiries involving a minimum of formalization. Now we return to some recent work that puts heavy emphasis on formalization and mathematization. This work cuts across many of the conventional behavioral science disciplines, although at least one stimulus for many of the procedures employed comes from economics. We will look at some of the issues raised in economics, game theory, decision theory, and related areas.

That work has a wide range, and it is often complex and highly technical. Hence there will be no attempt even to summarize all the main themes, and I will avoid consideration of the details of the formal structures proposed. Since the *raison d'etre* of many of the inquiries in this area is precisely to develop such symbolized structures, it may seem strange to exclude their consideration. The reason for doing so is that my concern is not with the "inner workings" of the models, formal structures, etc., that are proposed, but with their import for the scientific study and measurement of behavior.

Given that goal, one important question is the linkage of the

115

formal structures to observable behavior; many controversial issues about that linkage are relevant to this book. As a warning for those who are generally unfamiliar with the work here discussed, it should be emphasized that no one "school" is involved, that there are many hotly disputed statements among those who accept, say, the general merits of a game theory approach, and that it would be a serious distortion to take the comments made here as necessarily applicable to all or even most workers in this area. Since many of my comments are negative, it should also be emphasized that the mathematical abilities and ingenuity of many of the people mentioned are impressive, and no disparagement of their formalizing skills or talents is intended.

B. PURPOSES OF FORMALIZATION

Many different and conflicting accounts of what is achievable through formalization can be found. As we shall see throughout this chapter, there has been considerable controversy as to the extent any given formal model can be used to describe behavior as contrasted to the extent that it prescribes how a given type of person *should* behave in some given situation. The work of Davidson, McKinsey, and Suppes will be discussed in this section as an interesting account of one view of what the function of formalization is and also as a device for illustrating something of the flavor one often encounters in efforts of this kind. They say:

> "We take it as the general function of formal value theory to provide formal criteria for rational decision, choice and evaluation. Our conception of this aspect of value theory is in one way similar to Kant's, for like him we believe it possible to state in purely formal terms certain necessary conditions for rationality with respect to value. Unlike Kant, however, we do not suggest that any particular evaluations or value principles can be derived from purely formal considerations. Value theory, as here conceived, is associated with another venerable, and at present rather unfashionable, tradition, for it seems to us that there is a sense in which it is perfectly correct to say that just as logic can be used to define necessary formal conditions for rational

belief, so it is a use of value theory to define necessary formal conditions for rational choice."[1]

(In Sections E and F below the question of what constitutes a "rational" decision is discussed further.)

In developing their formal theory, the authors consider a set of alternatives, called K, that are to be ranked in order of preference. 'P' stands for 'is preferred to,' and is taken as a transitive and asymmetrical relation. In their symbolism, 'x P y' stands for the fact that x is preferred to y. When two alternatives are equivalent in preference, the relation is called E (and is regarded as transitive and symmetrical). They then offer the following as a partial explication of a rational preference ranking:

> "*Definition 1. The ordered triple* <K, P, E> *is a*
> RATIONAL PREFERENCE RANKING *if and only if:*
> P1. *The relation P is transitive;*
> P2. *The relation E is transitive;*
> P3. *If* x *and* y *are in* K, *then exactly one of the following:*
>   x P y, y P x, x E y."[2]

The authors go on to say that the definition just given "at best provides necessary conditions for rational ranking," since obviously many phenomena that meet the criteria of an RPR (rational preference ranking) as given in Definition 1 have nothing to do with preference or value. But they believe Definition 1 does provide some necessary conditions and therefore that it can "serve as a basis for partial explication of rationality in the field of value."

Definition 1 sets no limitation on the kind of entities to be ordered, and there is no need to take the members of K as mutually exclusive or as exhaustive alternatives (although they may be.) The definition also is "neutral" as to when or under what conditions an alternative is preferred or equivalent to another. They draw analogies to the syllogism, and say that Definition 1 is "as indifferent to particular rankings between

---

[1]Donald Davidson, J. C. C. McKinsey, and Patrick Suppes, *Outlines of a Formal Theory of Value*, I, Stanford, Academic Reprints, 1954, p. 2.
[2]*Ibid.*, p. 6.

pairs as the theory of the syllogism is to the truth of individual premises." In addition, just as the "universal validity of syllogistic inference" has no implication for the status of its premises, so the "universal applicability" of Definition 1 has no implication that value judgments are "objective, or absolute, or timeless."

But still, they go on, Definition 1 "is intended to perform a normative function." They say:

> "If a, b and c are alternatives, for example, and a P b and b P c, then in an RPR it follows that a P c. This cannot be taken simply as a description of how people order their preferences; on any normal interpretation of preference, we would expect to find cases where people preferred a to b, b to c, and c to a. By refusing to call such a pattern of preferences *rational* we in effect establish a formal condition for rationality. . . . It would be misleading to interpret the definition as saying that if a P b and b P c, the a *should* be preferred to c. The definition allows us to deduce no normative statements from non-normative premises; it does not *say* what we should believe, prefer, or choose."[3]

What then, is the normative function of the definition, if it does not tell us what should be preferred under a given set of circumstances? (In later sections, we shall see that other writers do take their models as prescribing what a rational man should choose under specific circumstances.) Again an analogy is made to formal logic. If X is a consequence of Y, and Y of Z, then X is a consequence of Z. "Logic does not say that we should reason in accordance with this truth, nor that if we believe the antecedent of the sample truth, we should believe the consequent." But, they say, we use such a logical truth "to explain what we mean in part by reasoning rationally," which is a normative use of a logical truth. In short, as I understand the authors, they are saying that just as one cannot reject the conclusion of a valid syllogism without being inconsistent, so one cannot reject a P c (given a P b and b P c) without being somehow inconsistent.

They then turn to discussing three axioms of Definition 1, which they believe "embody necessary conditions for a rational pattern of preferences." We will look only at the first axiom,

---

[3]*Ibid.*, p. 8.

which provides that in an RPR, if x is valued more than y, and y more than z, then x is valued more than z. They discuss a possible serious difficulty raised by the following example: A teacher is offered a choice of three jobs by a cynical administrator—(a) a full professorship at a salary of $5000, (b) an associate professorship at a salary of $5500, and (c) an assistant professorship at $6000. The teacher decides that a P b since the rank outweighs the small salary differential; that b P c for the same reason, but that c P a because the salary differential is now great enough to make up for the lower rank.

The authors argue that this is an irrational set of preferences. Even though the reason for each of the paired comparisons may be good, such a set of preferences would make a "rational choice" impossible. They say that for a given set of alternatives and preferences, a rational choice selects either the alternative that is preferred to all the others, or, if there are several equivalent alternatives preferred to all the others, any of those equivalents. "In short, a rational choice is one which selects an alternative to which none is preferred." But in the example above, whatever alternative is chosen there is another that is preferred to it, and so no rational choice is possible.[4]

The authors also discuss several types of "strong" measurement in addition to the "weak" measurement exemplified by an RPR. The strongest is what they call an *absolute* scale (as in the cardinality of classes), in which the "uniqueness characteristic" is said to be "absolutely unique"; the next strongest is the *ratio* scale (as in mass and length), in which the uniqueness characteristic is an arbitrary unit; the next is the *interval* scale (as in measurement of longitude and time), in which the uniqueness characteristic is an arbitrary zero and unit. The RPR (the weakest of the four) is an *ordinal* scale, comparable to the Beaufort wind scale, and its uniqueness characteristic is that it is order preserving.

They then develop several alternative axiomatizations of a rational individual's preference pattern designed to show that preferences could be measured by an interval scale, instead of the

---

[4]*Ibid.*, pp. 9-10.

weak measurement that follows from Definition 1. They do not maintain that "any of these axiomatizations constitutes a completely adequate explication of any intuitive notion of rational preference," but hope that inquiring into the alternatives will help further progress.

We will not discuss Definitions 2, 3, and 4 here, but take note only of a final problem. All four definitions, they say, share an important limitation, viewed either as empirical hypotheses about actual preference patterns or as partial reconstructions of the formal aspects of the process through which rational judgments of relative value are made:

> "From a descriptive point of view, there is the patent falsehood that equivalence of preference is transitive, that is, that differences in preference can be infinitely discriminated. From the point of view of rational reconstruction, there is a failure to explicate the process by which, when two alternatives a and b are equivalent in felt preference, we may nevertheless sometimes rationally infer a difference in value (for example by noting a difference between the class of alternatives to which a is preferred and the class of alternatives to which b is preferred)."[5]

Looking ahead to their future work, they think that Definition 4 perhaps could be reasonably modified in a way that would eliminate the requirement of infinite discriminability.

In commenting on the work of Davidson, McKinsey, and Suppes, the first point I wish to make is that at least in a general way they proceed much as do other formalists in this area. Formalized structures are proposed that have some relation to certain types of behavior (decisions, values, preferences, etc.), but at least the initial formal structures, when compared to what is found empirically, are defective in that admittedly wrong assumptions are made, complex matters are oversimplified, etc. Thus Definition 1 is regarded as only a "partial explication," and all four definitions assume a "patent falsehood," that E is transitive. The models are then modified to become more isomorphic to the empirical area of concern.

---

[5]*Ibid.*, p. 40.

In my opinion, one great danger in such procedures is that often not enough warranted information is available about the empirical subject matter to judge the applicability of the model to what it supposedly is modeling, and this may lead to undue enthusiasm for a particular model. The usual kind of reply to such a criticism is that simply because a particular model is not useful for prediction does not show the whole approach is wrong; if, for example, similar criticisms had been directed against some work in the physical sciences, those areas might not have developed to the degree that they have.[6] I am not, of course, trying to argue against the usefulness of formal models in any area, but only trying to warn against *premature* celebrations of what has been accomplished.

Some attention also should be given to the analogy between logic and RPR's suggested by the authors. Do what they call "irrational" sets of preferences in fact generate the type of difficulties we face if we accept inconsistencies in logic? Here much depends, it seems to me, on what the person expressing his preferences is trying to say. Possibly in the example of the different academic ranks, the person faced with such a choice is not responding as "irrationally" as the authors assume.

What such a person might be expressing, in verbally reporting his preferences (a P b, b P c, c P a) is merely that those are his preferences when any two of the alternatives are compared, but that he simply has no preference when all three are simultaneously compared. In many situations, I see no need for even a rational individual to have a rational choice (taken as a choice to which no other alternative is preferred), if only because he has not yet made up his mind.

Another possibility is that an individual when considering *all three* alternatives prefers c to both the others, and then ranks a next and b last, but yet when looking at the possibilities one pair at a time has the preferences given in the example. Why call that irrational? Since we apparently are dealing with intuitive notions of rationality, I can only report that my "intuition" is

---

[6]See, for example, the comments by Eugene F. Elander, "Correspondence on Mathematical Models," *Social Science,* Vol. 37, 1962, p. 249.

that such preferences are not irrational. In any event, in the instance just described the individual has no difficulty in acting, nor is he uncertain or confused. Given all three alternatives at once, or given any two at a time, he has a clear preference; he is not in a Buridan's Ass situation.

Putting this another way, when "felt" preferences are involved, I suggest that some of the apparent incongruences or irrationalities may be more a function of the requirements of a given model than of any peculiarity in the individual whose preferences are being expressed. That preferences among pairs of alternatives taken separately are somehow inconsistent with a preference among all those alternatives considered simultaneously does not, as far as I can see, have the "dire" consequences that the acceptance of inconsistencies in logic may have. Such "inconsistent" preferences may be galling to the enthusiastic formalist who finds it hard to develop models for those preferences, but we do have a saying that there is no accounting for tastes.

We should also bear in mind that many types of scientific inquiry into "irrational" preferences (including their measurement) are possible. We can inquire into the circumstances under which preferences such as a P b, b P c, c P a arise, for example, as well as numerous related matters. As noted in Chapter IV, Catton found that clergymen did make comparisons of values that supposedly were incomparable. Many measurements of preference that may be useful in predicting behavior do not depend on a "rational" set of preferences.

Indeed, I believe that some writers on measurement overemphasize the importance of transitive asymmetrical relations in general. In Chapter II, Section D, the Mohs Scale of Hardness in mineralogy was discussed. The hardness of a mineral is measured by its ability to scratch, or be scratched by, one of a series of standard minerals arranged in order of increasing hardness. But, as critics of that scale point out, the relation *scratches* in this context is not transitive and asymmetrical, for two minerals neither of which can scratch the other can have different potentialities for scratching a third.

The scale is therefore defective in helping us ascertain certain kinds of information, but it is helpful in getting other kinds of information. The limitations of the scale suggest the desirability of developing a better one, but do not invalidate its usefulness for some purposes. And the limitations of the scale, from the point of view of its logical structure, may be no worse pragmatically than the nonformal limitations of other scales. "Irrationalities" in orderings, then, certainly do not necessarily preclude all possibility of measurement and in fact sometimes seem compatible with historically useful measurements.

C. UTILITIES AND THEIR MAXIMIZATION

In the literature on the type of formalized structures we are now considering, rational behavior is often closely related to the maximizing of utilities. The literature on utilities is extensive and diverse, and only certain aspects are taken up here.

In economic theory 'utility' was often used roughly as 'ability to satisfy a want,' or more formally, as the 'indicator of the level of want-gratification.' Jerome Rothenberg has given a helpful brief history of that notion. He says that in much traditional theory economic behavior is viewed as an attempt to maximize something; for consumers utility is posited as that which is being maximized. Rothenberg continues:

> "The concept of utility here has been a useful buffer between the action of choice and the supposed psychological ground of this action. By being able to speak of maximizing utility, the economist has not had to say that individuals try to maximize gratification, or satisfaction, or pleasure, or happiness, or virtue, etc., each one of which would seem to be making an empirical commitment in the field of psychology. Utility seems philosophically neutral, while the others seem to assert something about the substantive quality of the ultimate inner goad — if indeed it is unitary."[7]

_____

[7]Jerome Rothenberg, "Values and Value Theory in Economics," in Sherman Roy Krupp, ed., *The Structure of Economic Science,* Englewood Cliffs, Prentice-Hall, 1966, p. 227.

Whether this neutrality is really possible is another matter. I suggest that either implicit or explicit commitments are likely to be made. For example, Rothenberg says that economists tend to view the person as having a set of drives consisting of organic states disposing "him to activity aimed at reducing or transforming these same states in a way that leads to gratification." Drives "impose directionality on behavior," and indicate the instrumentalities through which the gratifying transformations can occur. This hardly seems neutral, since the emphasis is on organic, rather than on either environmental or biosocial, factors, and on "gratification" rather than on something else.

He goes on to say that if a person's preferences are structured so that he can give a complete transitive preference ordering of all the alternatives, we can describe his choices as if he had assigned different levels of utility to the alternatives and had selected the alternative(s) having the highest preference level of those available. Utility maximization, then, "refers almost entirely to the *structural* characteristics of preferences—namely, the presence or absence of complete preference orderings of alternatives."

In a recent article, Boulding discusses the choice process, and says that to describe such processes economists postulate a utility function in which every relevant state of the field is given an ordinal number indicating its order of preference. In a strong ordering, each state has a unique ordinal number; but in a weak ordering different states may have the same number. He continues:

> "As the economist sees it, then, the problem of valuation is that of ordering a field of choice and then selecting the first on the order of preference. This is the famous principle of maximizing behavior, as it is called, which is simply a mathematical elaboration of the rather obvious principle that people always do what seems to them best at the time. It has always surprised me, as I have remarked elsewhere, that such a seemingly empty principle should be capable of such enormous mathematical elaboration."[8]

---

[8]Kenneth E. Boulding, "The Emerging Superculture," in Kurt Baier and Nicholas Rescher, eds., *Values and the Future,* New York, Free Press, 1969, p. 337.

(In passing, we may note that far from being surprising that a nearly empty principle should permit enormous mathematical elaboration, it is precisely such "empty" principles that do allow such elaboration, as the history of much intellectual endeavor shows.)

Without intending any completeness at all in our survey, we have seen that there is a strong tendency to view utilities as logical constructs that somehow indicate want-gratifications through the ordering of preferences. From time to time, however, utilities are also taken as existing empirically.

Turning back now to measurement, Rothenberg mentions two traditions in utility measurement. The work of Thurstone and others in deriving an individual's preference scales and the von Neumann-Morgenstern axiomatization of utility theory under conditions of risk helped form one tradition, in which the search was for experimental techniques to measure utility functions. The second tradition stems from Paul Samuelson's "revealed preference" theory. Individual market behavior was focused on as the important observable, and preferences (the utility function) were "only logical entities useful for achieving logical closure of the system." The analytic task was construed as the postulation of the logically weakest assumptions about preference from which the properties of the observable market choices could be deduced. Rothenberg goes on:

> "There has been some linkage between the two traditions in measurement technique in connection with the quantification of Von Neumann-Morgenstern utility. An increasingly behavioristic interpretation of this utility concept has led essentially to the notion that Von Neumann-Morgenstern utility is simply a construct revealed by the pattern of observed risk choices. One important feature of this construct is that it is used for predictive purposes, not solely to achieve logical closure of the system."[9]

Boulding points out that to give content to the models, we must say what the preference field is and describe the preference function. If the field is made up of a set of possible exchanges

---

[9]Rothenberg, *op. cit.*, p. 239.

in a given system of exchange opportunities (prices), at least some properties of the function can be "deduced" from observing behavioral differences in response to different prices; i.e., the preferences are "revealed." In theory, if we can observe the individual's behavior under different price structures, we can determine his preference function, but in practice this is so difficult that what is observed is the aggregate behavior of many individuals under different price structures, "and we deduce from this some kind of aggregate or average preference function." Boulding concludes that there is some justification for so doing if "the preference functions of different individuals are not widely dissimilar."[10]

Boulding's remarks here perplex me. He apparently is saying that the main concern is the individual's preference function, but in practice we cannot observe that, so we observe group behavior instead and derive an aggregate preference function, but that this procedure is justified only if the preference functions (which we *cannot* observe) of the individuals making up the group are fairly similar. I suggest that warranted conclusions about group preferences may be useful even when we cannot observe individual preferences or when those individual preferences are dissimilar. As an even more radical suggestion, perhaps it would be more productive to forget about utilities and just investigate what can be observed.

This brings us back to an old problem about expressed preferences. Sometimes the emphasis is on what a "rational" ordering of preferences would be, and sometimes on "actual" preferences. When "actual" preferences are involved, one approach is to measure them through Thurstone-like techniques in which the respondent says what he would prefer under specified conditions. The other approach is to study the preferences the person (or group) exhibits among alternatives "in real life." The two sets of preferences may be similar or dissimilar; which we want to measure will depend on what behavior we want to predict.

10Boulding, *op. cit.*, p. 337.

D. COMMENTS ON MAXIMIZING UTILITIES

In my opinion, much of the literature on utilities and their maximization fluctuates between taking 'utility' simply as a logical construct useful for achieving closure in a formal model and taking it as designating something in behavior. This fluctuation comes about because one of the goals in this whole area of inquiry is to construct some formal models that either will describe or somehow illuminate human behavior.

To illustrate the logical closure aspect further, let us note what von Neumann and Morgenstern say about their treatment of utility:

> "We have treated the concept of utility in a rather narrow and dogmatic way. We have not only assumed that it is numerical — for which a tolerably good case can be made . . . but also that it is substitutable and unrestrictedly transferable between the various players. . . . We proceeded in this way for technical reasons: The numerical utilities were needed for the theory of the zero-sum two-person game — particularly because of the role that expectation values had to play in it. The substitutability and transferability were necessary for the theory of the zero-sum *n*-person game. . . ."[11]

They add that their notion should be modified and generalized, but foresaw definite difficulties in making those improvements.

At this point, we might note that sometimes formalists show a certain irritation when they find that human behavior does not follow the paths their models indicate. Frequently, they strive to modify the model suitably, but on occasion they feel so intuitively confident in the model that behavior deviating from it is "disposed of" as irrational. In any event, I think Rothenberg is correct when he described utility as intended to be a buffer between a choice and its supposed psychological ground. The use of utilities may enable the investigator to avoid direct inquiry into those grounds, but at the price of making utility a somewhat mysterious entity, especially since

---

[11]John von Neumann and Oskar Morgenstern, *Theory of Games and Economic Behavior,* 3rd ed., Princeton University Press, 1953, p. 604.

there is such reluctance to accept the utility as merely an artifact of a formal model.

If it is agreed that the subject of inquiry is the maximizing of something, what that something is becomes pertinent. Especially in the context of game theory, where the game may contain a numerical measure, care must be taken not to assume that a player's utility function is identical with that measure. As Luce and Raiffa point out:

> "For example, poker, when it is played for money, is a game with numerical payoffs assigned to each of the outcomes, and one way to play the game is to maximize one's expected money outcome. But there are players who enjoy the thrill of bluffing for its own sake, and they bluff with little or no regard to the expected payoff. Their utility functions cannot be identified with the game payments."[12]

In an attempt to overcome some of these problems, some writers on decision theory have been careful not to identify utility with the mathematical expectation of gain. Anatol Rapoport, for example, says that if people actually behaved according to mathematical expectation of gain in making decisions under conditions of risk, or if it were "intuitively obvious" that a rational person should make his decisions that way, then the theory of decisions under risk would reduce itself to the computation of mathematical expectations. But, he says, not only do people usually not make decisions that way, often they should not; the mathematical expectation of a person buying fire insurance is negative, but that person still may be wise to purchase it.

He goes on to note that in decision theory models utility assignments are made that are not necessarily proportional to the amount of gain expected, and also subjective probabilities (the individual's estimate of probability which may be quite different from "objective" probability) are postulated. But if the decision theory model is supposed to be descriptive, we have

[12]R. Duncan Luce and Howard Raiffa, *Games and Decisions*, New York, Wiley, 1957, p. 5.

to know how to infer the utilities and the subjective probabilities "on the basis of which the decisions will appear consistent and predictable." He then says:

> "But posing the problem in this way reveals the strong tacit assumption that behavior of individuals or of classes of individuals *is* consistent and predictable, once the underlying utilities and subjective probabilities of the alternatives are uncovered; i.e., it is assumed that such utilities and probabilities *exist.* And this may by no means be the case. There may be chance factors governing decisions, for example, chance reversals of preferences or chance fluctuations in probability estimates (depending, perhaps, on what aspect of the situation is in the focus of attention)."[13]

Scodel, Ratoosh, and Minas have described much of the work in this field. According to them, formalists often begin with a notion such as the maximization of expected utility, and then attempt to explain why the behavior of the experimental subjects deviates from the norms of the model. They say a "principal difficulty" in such work is that assumptions are made which involve a product of utility and subjective probability, when neither is known. If utility is taken to be a linear function of money, and subjective probability is equated to "objective" probability, it is easy to construct a theoretical model for predicting decisions, but such models "are extremely poor in making predictions about the way persons actually behave in risk-taking situations."[14]

In view of the "deviant" responses found when actual behavior is studied, the authors felt it would be useful to "examine the influence of personality variables." In their study of decision making in a dice game, they gave the subjects an IQ test (Wechsler), the Thematic Apperception Test, and the Allport-Vernon-Lindzey Study of Values test, among others. Some of their findings were : 1) In determining betting preferences, ex-

---

13Anatol Rapoport, "Introduction," in Dorothy Willner, ed., *Decisions, Values and Groups,* Vol. 1, New York, Pergamon Press, 1960, p. xv.

14Alvin Scodel, Philburn Ratoosh, and J. Sayer Minas, "Some Personality Correlates of Decision Making Under Conditions of Risk," in Dorothy Willner, *op. cit.,* p. 37.

pected dollar value has negligible importance; 2) Intelligence was significantly related to variability in risk-taking, but not to the degree of risk-taking; 3) High payoff subjects scored higher on the Allport-Vernon-Lindzey *theoretical* and *aesthetic* values and lower on the *economic, social,* and *political* values than the low payoff subjects (within the college group; other subjects were not given this test); and 4) The low payoff group scored higher on need achievement as measured in the TAT than the high payoff group. They characterize their results as "far from overwhelming," but as pointing to the importance of personality variables in risk-taking behavior.[15]

Without denigrating the findings of these authors, it may be pointed out that there are some problems with the use of projective techniques and the Allport-Vernon-Lindzey values test and that in a sense we may have taken the long road home. If we find utility somewhat elusive in the beginning, to attempt to learn more about it through the use of personality tests may not be particularly productive.

Such issues, in my opinion, are also connected with important methodological issues in behavioral science. As mentioned earlier, Rothenberg suggested that some workers were attracted to the notion of utility because it seemed "neutral," whereas an attempt to talk instead about maximizing satisfaction, or pleasure, etc., would seem "to assert something about the substantive quality of the ultimate inner goad—if indeed, it is unitary." I suggest the fundamental mistake here is to assume an ultimate and inner goad, unitary or not. The tendency to separate sharply man from his environment, mind from body, and "inner" and "outer" in behavior, although deeply entrenched in our intellectual tradition, has given rise to a great many methodogenic difficulties and problems. A transactional approach which does not assume separates that somehow have to come together and affect each other seems much more adequate, and does not have as a consequence that we must postulate either some mysterious ultimate inner goad or an equally mysterious "neutral" utility.

---

[15]*Ibid.*, p. 48.

E. RATIONAL BEHAVIOR

In game theory, decision theory, formal value theory, some aspects of economics, etc., strong emphasis is put on the notion of "rational" behavior. For example, Arrow remarks that both theoretical economists and other social theorists frequently postulate that the individual or group whose behavior is being investigated is seeking to maximize some quantity. To illustrate, in the theory of the firm, economists may postulate that an individual searches for the type of operation that will yield more profit than any other alternative, and then christen such behavior as "rational."[16]

Sometimes, as mentioned when the work of Davidson, McKinsey, and Suppes was discussed, rationality is construed in terms of a kind of consistency in preference ordering. Other conditions also may be added. For example, Helmer and Rescher establish four conditions for calling a person "rational" (under certain circumstances): 1) In contexts such as betting, the rational man has mutually consistent preferences, or at least is willing to correct those inconsistencies that are brought to his attention; 2) He maintains reasonably stable personal probabilities as long as no new relevant evidence is available; 3) When new relevant evidence is made known, he changes his personal probabilities in the appropriate way; 4) In simple cases in which the degree of confirmation of an hypothesis on the basis of known evidence is ascertained, the personal probability of the rational person concerning that hypothesis conforms reasonably to the degree of confirmation; in particular, he is indifferent as to which side he chooses in "fair" bets.[17]

In game theory, it is sometimes assumed that a rational player not only is striving to maximize utility, but that he is fully informed of the preference patterns of all the other players, and is aware of other aspects of the particular game being played. Luce and Raiffa emphasize both the different uses of 'rational' in

---

[16]Kenneth Arrow, "Mathematical Models in the Social Sciences," *General Systems*, Vol. 1, 1956, p. 33.

[17]Olaf Helmer and Nicholas Rescher, *On the Epistemology of the Inexact Sciences*, Santa Monica, The RAND Corp., P-1513, 1958, p. 26.

different theories and that often the assumptions made do not conform to what can be observed:

> "Though it is not apparent from some writings, the term 'rational' is far from precise, and it certainly means different things in the different theories that have been developed. Loosely, it seems to include any assumption one makes about the players maximizing something, and any about complete knowledge on the part of the player in a very complex situation, where experience indicates that a human being would be far more restricted in his perceptions."[18]

The connection between *utility* and *rationality*, then, varies from theory to theory, although in the general research area we are now considering the two are intertwined. It seems fair to say that for many workers in this field there is a kind of tension between their endeavor to elucidate or explicate some intuitive notion of rationality they believe is important and perhaps widely shared, and their attempt to use 'rational' in a way conforming to some observed behavioral sequences.

To illustrate, Kenneth Arrow assumes that a rational individual is one whose behavior conforms to his Axioms I and II. In his discussion 'x is preferred or indifferent to y' is symbolized by '$x \ R \ y$'. Axiom I is: *"For all x and y, either $x \ R \ y$ or $y \ R \ x$."* Axiom II is: *"For all x, y, and z, $x \ R \ y$ and $y \ R \ z$ imply $x \ R \ z$."* He then says that although the "concept of rationality used throughout this study is at the heart of modern economic analysis" and has "great intuitive appeal," it has its difficulties. For example, one of its consequences is that "the choice to be made from any set of alternatives can be determined by the choices made between pairs of alternatives," but sometimes behaviorally we are offered not choices between pairs, but many alternatives.[19]

Complications are compounded when an attempt is made to move from individual rational behavior to rational social behavior, as Arrow does. He sees the general problem as the con-

---

[18]Luce and Raiffa, *op. cit.*, p. 5.

[19]Kenneth J. Arrow, *Social Choice and Individual Values*, 2nd ed., New York, Wiley, 1963, p. 13, pp. 19-20.

struction of an ordering relation for "society as a whole" that will satisfy his Axioms I and II. His work has stimulated considerable controversy, especially his conclusion that the plausible requirements for what is often called a "social welfare function" are incompatible, and hence that such a function is impossible.

Arrow maintains that the utilities of different individuals are not commensurable, holding that "interpersonal comparison of utilities has no meaning and, in fact, that there is no meaning relevant to welfare comparisons in the measurability of individual utility."[20] As he sets up the problem, he mentions that in some methods of social choice, such as a dictatorship, there can be a rational choice; "rational in the sense that any individual can be rational in his choices." The question, then, is can "such consistency be attributed to collective modes of choice, where the wills of many people are involved?" His study is concerned only with the formal aspects of that question; he is interested in whether or not it is formally possible to construct a procedure, subject to certain "natural" conditions, that will allow us to move from a set of known individual tastes (values) to social decision making.

To illustrate the problem, Arrow refers to the famous paradox of voting. For this purpose, he assumes "the traditional identification of rationality with maximization of some sort," and says that community rational behavior would mean that the community orders certain alternatives according to its collective preferences "once for all" and chooses the alternative that is highest in preference from among those available. An apparently plausible way of ascertaining the collective preference scale would be through paired comparisons. But this can generate a paradox reminiscent of the one discussed earlier concerning different academic ranks.

For example, assume a community of just three voters, and that this community must choose among three alternatives. Assume further that the first individual prefers A to B and B to C, and hence prefers A to C; that the second individual prefers B to C and C to A, and hence B to A, and the third person

---

[20]*Ibid.*, p. 9.

prefers C to A and A to B, and hence C to B. Then, two people (a majority of the community) prefer A to B, and two people (a majority) prefer B to C, and hence the community seems to prefer A to C. But two people (again a majority) indicated that they preferred C to A. Arrow says: "So the method . . . for passing from individual to collective tastes fails to satisfy the condition of rationality, as we ordinarily understand it."[21] His book is a technical discussion of possible *other* ways of aggregating individual tastes that will yield rational social behavior (i.e., a social welfare function).

Arrow argues that there are several plausible requirements for such an aggregation. For example, if a particular alternative is preferred to another by all members of the social group, then it should be preferred in the social preference ranking. Another is that no dictator should have the power to determine the social preference regardless of the preferences of the other individuals. Arrow goes on to show that if all his plausible conditions are met, there *cannot* be a social welfare function, for the conditions are incompatible.[22]

Some commentators were very impressed by Arrow's results, while others were not so impressed. At the very least, the judgment of the significance of his work will depend on how seriously one takes the conditions he has discussed. Some writers, for example, have argued that one of his postulates ("Independence of Irrelevant Alternatives") can be dropped, for they believe that the extraneous alternatives are not really irrelevant.[23] Such criticisms of Arrow are likely to assume that his fundamental approach is worthwhile; other critics may find that approach less productive. It is worth noting that Arrow, after mentioning some of the difficulties in his notion of rationality, suggests the possibility that a "broader concept of rationality" might resolve the paradox he emphasizes in his book.

We have seen, then a variety of themes emphasized in for-

---

[21]*Ibid.*, pp. 2-3.

[22]Many of these requirements are stated in a highly technical way by Arrow. A less technical and symbolized version is given in Nicholas Rescher, *Introduction to Value Theory*, Englewood Cliffs, Prentice-Hall, 1969, pp. 101-102.

[23]*Ibid.*, pp. 102 ff.; Luce and Raiffa, *op. cit.*, pp. 340 ff.

mal approaches relying on the notion of rationality: rationality has been taken as a kind of consistency and stability in preferences, as the maximizing of a quantity, as a willingness to alter personal probabilities in the direction of the evidence, as having complete information about the preference patterns of others involved in some social transaction, and as some combination of such themes. Normally, these emphases are viewed as in conformity with some intuitive and widely held notion of rationality.

F. COMMENTS ON RATIONALITY

From the point of view of the scientific measurement of values, we seem quickly to encounter a mare's nest when we try to thread our way through the literature on rationality. One difficulty is that often authors use some such phrase as how "we ordinarily understand rationality" and then try to formalize that ordinary understanding. In my opinion, 'rationality' belongs to that group of terms for which it is extremely difficult to specify just what is ordinarily intended by the term; even if that can be ascertained, what scientific warrant there may be for that use is not discussed.

Moreover, there seems to be little support offered for the notion that preferences should be rational, in whatever sense of 'rational' a given author adopts. Especially when preferences are taken as tastes, what basis is there for assuming that in some sense they should be consistent, or reasoned, or rational? To answer such questions, we need better specifications for the terminology than we are normally given.

More generally, often there is unclarity as to the basic use of the formal models offered. Sometimes the hope is expressed that they will be useful for predicting behavior, but then we run into the problem that observed behavior so often deviates from what the model predicts. On the other hand, if rational behavior is somehow supposed to be a better way of acting (to prescribe preferences or choices that should be made), we run into other problems; the putative goal may be achieved more easily or efficiently than in the "rational" way postulated in some particular model.

Just what 'normative' or 'prescriptive' refer to in such contexts can be problematic. For example, Robert L. Davis describes the use of 'rational man' and 'normative' as unfortunate. He says that perhaps the first theorists to use such terms intended to develop a framework that would tell a rational man what he should do, but in recent theories a far more modest aim is involved, for rational behavior is merely whatever behavior satisfies the requirements of the model constructed. Davis goes on:

> "For instance, the theory of zero-sum two-person games can be taken as normative theory in the sense that it gives instructions according to which a man will be able to maximize his expected payoff in such a game, assuming he can find the solution. But this does not say anyone should use this theory in playing an actual game: it may be that he can more easily secure this maximum expected payoff in some other way. . . ."[24]

I suspect that a partial motive for some work in this area is the view that somehow values (utilities, preferences, etc.) cannot be measured unless they are rational. But that seems mistaken; considerable progress can be expected in ascertaining the circumstances under which individuals or groups do express certain preferences, and the type of "rationality" necessary to enable scientific inquiry to proceed will be the kind of "if . . . then" links found between the expression of a preference and its conditions, rather than in some type of consistency among an individual's preferences.

In any event, worthy of notice is the fact that often in the development of a model for rational behavior the author finds that he has had to make incorrect assumptions, oversimplify, or neglect what seem to be the important factors. We have mentioned some such examples earlier; now some comments of Arrow are appropriate. Early in his book he emphasized that his investigation of the formal aspects of "collective social choice" left out

---

[24] R. M. Thrall, C. H. Coombs, and R. L. Davis, eds., *Decision Processes*, New York, Wiley, 1954, pp. 4-5.

some important aspects. First are the game aspects (both in the popular sense and in the technical sense of game theory); for example, no consideration is given to the enjoyment of the decision process; e.g., to the desire to play and win. Further, Arrow assumes throughout that "individual values are taken as data and are not capable of being altered by the nature of the decision process itself," which he says may be "unreal."[25] In view of the behavioral science materials showing how values (in some sense) can indeed be affected by the "decision process," the "unreality" of that assumption seems evident.

G.   CONCLUSION

What can be said about the general aim of the type of formalized model building discussed in this chapter? There are still those who see the models as useful in predicting behavior, more or less in the spirit of von Neumann and Morgenstern. They were interested in the problem of finding "an exact description" of economic behavior, and hoped to establish that "the typical problems of economic behavior become strictly identical with the mathematical notions of suitable games of strategy." More and more, apparently, such a *descriptive* function for the models is being eschewed, since the results are so often disappointing when the models are tested against observable behavior. A fairly typical statement comes from Suppes and Atkinson, who did test some game theory models: "it is possible to view game theory as a descriptive, empirical theory of behavior, but in fact this does not seem to be a very promising approach."[26]

Many writers emphasize that the models are *prescriptive* in the sense of describing how people should behave. That theme is also found in von Neumann and Morgenstern, who suggest that rational behavior has a "superiority . . . over any other kind" of behavior. And Rapoport insists that game theory is "definitely

---

25Arrow, *Social Choice and Individual Values*, pp. 6-8.

26Von Neumann and Morgenstern, *op. cit.*, p. 1, p. 2. Patrick Suppes and Richard C. Atkinson, *Markov Learning Models for Multiperson Interactions*, Stanford, Stanford University Press, 1960, p. 33.

normative in spirit and method." He goes on to say that its goal "is a *prescription* of how a rational player should behave" in games in which the preferences of the players are given in utility units.[27]

And yet there frequently is a feeling that perhaps with some modification some such models could be useful for prediction, because the assumptions upon which they are based are so plausible. For example, Robert H. Strotz comments on the "strong intuitive appeal" some game theory axioms have. Although he admits the possibility that a person might act inconsistently with those axioms, he believes that "every normal person" would be inclined to accept them as precepts and that it "would be a strange man indeed" who would continue violating them once he clearly understood what he was violating.[28] If the various assumptions made in a given theory are as well founded as Strotz thinks they are, then the difference between the "rational" person and an ordinary mortal may not be so great after all.

Another possible approach is to view the models as normative, not in the sense of saying how people should behave, but as illuminating what is meant "by reasoning rationally" (e.g., unless a person has a preference ordering such that he chooses an alternative to which no other available alternative is preferred, a "rational choice" is impossible).

From the point of view of the measurement of observed behavior, all of these approaches (descriptive, prescriptive, normative) run into difficulties, or so I have argued. It therefore seems to me that either the formal models must be improved in terms of the predictions they facilitate or that a more convincing explanation must be given of the scientific usefulness of normative models.

One reason the models are so poor in predicting behavior is that they usually are so heavily and predominantly deductive. As W. K. Estes has noted, in this respect game theory and deci-

---

[27]Von Neumann and Morgenstern, *op. cit.*, p. 32. Anatol Rapoport, *Fights, Games, and Debates,* Ann Arbor, University of Michigan Press, 1960, pp. 226-227.

[28]Robert H. Strotz, "Cardinal Utility," *American Economic Review,* Vol. XLIII, 1953, pp. 391-393.

sion theory are much like earlier deductive systems of ethics. He remarks that in studies of human choices the "elaboration of theory has far outrun the front line of empirical investigation," and that a common pattern is first to select a "preferred type of theory" and then to look for empirical support. He advocates much closer attention to observed data and the introduction of hypotheses as needed to describe and predict the data.[29]

In addition, I would emphasize that there are serious terminological and methodological problems (often intermixed) involved in many of the basic problems considered in this general area of inquiry. To illustrate, I will take two examples from Arrow.

In discussing the impossibility of an "interpersonal comparison of utility," he says that "it seems to make no sense to add the utility of one individual, a psychic magnitude in his mind, with the utility of another individual."[30] This seems to imply a strong kind of mentalism, a location within a mind, and other debatable psychological assumptions. Insofar as I understand such a mentalism, I agree that it would preclude interpersonal comparisons, but if we do not accept that type of approach, the comparisons may be possible. Some (not all, of course) writers in this area persevere in quite unscientific approaches to many of the basic elements in their whole inquiry.

Second, in his discussion of some implications of the work of von Neumann and Morgenstern, Arrow says:

> "The point here, broadly speaking, is that, once a machinery for making social choices from individual tastes is established, individuals will find it profitable, from a rational point of view, to misrepresent their tastes by their actions, either because such misrepresentation is somehow directly profitable or, more usually, because some other individual will be made so much better off by the first individual's misrepresentation that he could compensate the first individual in such a way that both are better off than if everyone really acted in direct accordance with his

---

[29]W. K. Estes, "A Descriptive Approach to the Dynamics of Choice Behavior," *Behavioral Science,* Vol. 6, 1961, pp. 178-179.

[30]Arrow, *Social Choice and Individual Values,* p. 11.

tastes. Thus, in an electoral system based on plurality voting, it is notorious that an individual who really favors a minor party candidate will frequently vote for the less undesirable of the two major party candidates rather than 'throw away his vote.' "[31]

He goes on to say that the problem is to devise rules for a game so that individuals "will actually express their true tastes even when they are acting rationally."

I find Arrow's use of the term 'misrepresentation' peculiar. If I would very much like to see a third party candidate elected, but believe he has no chance at all of winning, and find one of the major party candidates better than the other and therefore vote for him, how have I misrepresented my tastes? If I buy a $30,000 house rather than the $50,000 one I would like more but cannot afford, I haven't misrepresented my preferences unless one insists on a quixotic use of terminology. Or, in a game, I might seemingly misrepresent my "true tastes" for some reason, but that is another preference — I do not act in accord with a particular preference I have because of some other preference I have. If I understand Arrow correctly, the issue here is not simply one of a possible careless use of words, but something more serious about the "true" nature of tastes. In any event, in this whole area we often find heavy reliance on terms for which it is extremely difficult to locate the referent.

My final point is that whether we take preferences, utilities, or something else as central to values, we seem to come back to many of the questions discussed earlier in this book, most importantly those concerned with the need for a coherent statement of what it is we are supposedly talking about. For example, if 'value' is identified with 'preference,' do we mean preference as exhibited in a questionnaire or rank-ordering procedure, or do we mean that the person would choose in the way he has said he would, or something else? Or if 'preference' is taken not as identical to 'value,' but as related to it, other issues arise. Perhaps, for example, no harm is done if preferences are inconsistent in some sense, so long as values are consistent.[32]

---

[31]*Ibid.*, p. 7.
[32]For one such discussion, see Rescher, *op. cit.*, pp. 109 ff.

I am not denying, of course, that formalized models may prove very helpful at some point, nor am I maintaining that at present they are worthless. Rather I am suggesting that all too often their *present* merits are exaggerated, and that in some quarters, at least, writers proceed almost as if any formalization must be a gain.

Chapter VII

VALUES AS OBJECTS OF INTERESTS AND AS SELECTIVE SYSTEMS

A. PRELIMINARY COMMENTS

This chapter is devoted to a discussion of the ways in which values are measurable according to the theories developed by Ralph B. Perry and Stephen C. Pepper. Their approach to values has historical continuity with utilitarian and hedonistic ethical theories, as contrasted to other-worldly, religious, and intuitionist views. Both authors place considerable emphasis on incorporating relevant scientific findings about human behavior into their value theories. Unlike many contemporary Anglo-American philosophers, Perry and Pepper focus much more on valuating behavior than they do on the "logic" of value discourse. In terms of conventional categories, both theories are empirical, naturalistic, and cognitivist. Although the point of view characteristic of Perry and Pepper is regarded by many analytic philosophers as misdirected and outmoded, I believe it deserves careful consideration.

B. PERRY'S INTEREST THEORY

Perry's work in value theory covered a long time span, although his basic approach remained relatively unchanged. Some of the themes occurring in his early *The Moral Economy* (1909) were developed in much more detail in *General Theory of Value*

(1926), and were further developed and applied to the major institutions of our civilization in *Realms of Value* (1954). Although Perry became somewhat more "naturalistic" as his views developed, even in his earlier formulations he insisted on regarding morality in humanistic, this-worldly, empirical terms. In his first book he described "the nucleus of morality" as "the precipitate of mankind's prolonged experiment in living," and in his last book he says morality "arises from the universal human situation, in which man finds himself confronted by the necessity of reconciling conflicting interests."[1]

Perry's interest theory of value can be viewed as having three foci: (1) Interests as basic to value; (2) The organization of interests into an economy; and (3) Harmonious happiness as the fundamental standard of morality.

(1) Interests. The key to Perry's value theory is the view that anything whatever is a value in the elementary or generic sense if it is the object of any interest whatever.[2] He began by viewing an interest as a "unit of life," and described it as "essentially an organization which consistently acts for its own preservation." An elaborate account of interests was given in *General Theory of Value*. Perry differentiated his view from those making 'interest' equivalent to 'attention,' for he wanted to include desires and dispositions as well. He emphasized the tendency of organisms to favor some things and to disfavor others, including the tendency to conserve or create what is favored and to prevent or destroy what is disfavored. 'Interest' names the *"state, act, attitude or disposition of favor or disfavor."* In *Realms of Value* Perry describes an interest as *"a train of events determined by expectation of its outcome,"* and says:

> "... the word 'interest' is the least misleading name for a certain class of acts or states which have the common characteristic of *being for or against*.... 'Interest,' then, is to be taken as a class name for such names as 'liking'-'disliking,' 'loving'-'hating,'

---

[1] Ralph B. Perry, *The Moral Economy*, New York, Scribner's, 1909, pp. 7-8; *Realms of Value*, Cambridge, Harvard University Press, 1954, p. 430.

[2] R. B. Perry, *General Theory of Value*, Cambridge, Harvard University Press, 1926, p. 116; *Realms of Value*, p. 3.

'hoping'-'fearing,' 'desiring'-'avoiding,' and countless other kindred names."[3]

Perry also developed elaborate analyses of the possible types of relation between 'value' and 'interest.' Perhaps his fundamental argument was that an identification of 'generic value' with 'any object of any interest' is the hypothesis or "descriptive definition" that best accounts for the data to be explained. Taking interest as the center of reference helps to make "the data and the perplexities denoted by 'good' and 'evil,' 'right' and 'wrong,' 'better' and 'worse,' or grouped within the special fields of morality, art, religion and kindred institutions" fall into place and "form a comprehensive system."[4]

(2) The Organization of Interests. As the title of his first book illustrates, Perry was keenly interested in the organization of interests into an "economy." The starting point there was a simple interest. Such interests are all on a par; none are too humble to count, and none have a privileged place. But a fundamental characteristic of life is that not all interests can be satisfied, for interests may conflict both within the behavior of one person and within group settings. Thus an organization or economy of interests is necessary. Moral goodness, as contrasted to simple goodness, "must be determined with reference to nothing less than the totality of all affected interests," and is "simply the greatest possible good, where good . . . means any object of interest whatsoever."[5]

In *General Theory of Value,* Perry discusses "the critique of value," or how *generic* values themselves are to be evaluated. Three criteria *(intensity, preference,* and *inclusiveness)* are quantitative and will be discussed in the next section. The fourth, *correctness,* is nonquantitative, for it does not lead to a judgment of *comparative* value. Correctness is involved in the truth or falsity of the judgment upon which an interest is based. For example, if someone prizes a painting on the incorrect supposi-

---

[3]*The Moral Economy,* p. 11; *General Theory of Value,* p. 115; *Realms of Value,* p. 3, p. 7.

[4]*General Theory of Value,* p. 126. See also *Realms of Value,* p. 13.

[5]*The Moral Economy,* pp. 52-66, p. 72.

tion that it is by Titian, he may prize it less when he finds out that Titian was not the painter. The object of an incorrect interest (in this sense) is not necessarily less valuable than the object of a correct interest. A person unaware of his error may persist in his "mistaken" interests, and these interests generate value as much as any other interest. But when the mistake is found out, the interest may be weakened.[6]

A main purpose of Perry's account of the organization of interests is to differentiate between 'generic value' and 'moral value.' He was criticized again and again on the ground that his identification of 'value' with 'any object of any interest' must be erroneous, for clearly many things that are valuable according to his theory are morally bad. An irony of this criticism is that Perry was as concerned as his critics were that various actual interests be morally condemned. So from the beginning in one way or another he differentiated between 'moral value' and 'generic value.'

Generic value is produced by the satisfaction of any interest, including bad interests, but moral value involves fulfillment of an organization of interests. Not only may some interests be morally bad, but some good interests may have to be deferred or subordinated to other interests, and some objects of a good interest similarly may be subordinated to other objects of that interest. Typical of his approach is the following comment on drug addiction:

> "While the craving does invest its object with positive value, the craving may be invested with negative value from the standpoint of other interests; and this second value may be considered as overruling the positive value owing to its taking the higher ground of health or morals. The appetitive goodness of the drug does not include or imply the hygienic or moral goodness of the appetite."[7]

(3) Harmonious happiness. On the theory as stated so far, there are many ways in which interests could be organized and

---

[6]*General Theory of Value*, pp. 612-615.

[7]*Realms of Value*, p. 11. See also *The Moral Economy*, pp. 13-15; *General Theory of Value*, p. 137.

judged comparatively. Although in his earlier work **Perry** also devoted attention to such issues, his clearest statement is in *Realms of Value,* where "harmonious happiness" is taken as the basic criterion for morality. He says:

> "The moral good has been defined as harmonious happiness, or as that organization of interests in which each enjoys the non-interference and support of the others, whether within the personal life or the life of society. This becomes the moral 'first principle.' It sets the standard by which objects are deemed morally good or bad, and is the premise from which right, duty and virtue are to be derived."[8]

At least three questions arise about harmonious happiness: In what does it consist? Does its introduction achieve what Perry wants it to achieve? What is the weight of the evidence adduced by Perry in its support?

Perry says that his emphasis is more on *harmony* than on *happiness.* He takes happiness, not as pleasure (in the sense of somatic sensation) but as "positivity of interest," and not as an attribute of one interest, but as an "attribute of the total person." Happiness, then, refers to the *"general auspiciousness* of a person's life." He reiterates that the function of morality is to remove conflict and thus to facilitate forms of happiness that are mutually enhancing. He argues that it is not so much the business of value theory to spell out what constitutes happiness as it is to remove conflicts that will generate unhappiness.[9]

In my opinion, the introduction of this "first principle" does do what Perry wants done within his value theory. Since the whole dynamics of his system rests on the removal of conflict (the achievement of harmony), taking "harmonious happiness" as a major criterion for judging values follows naturally enough; in a sense it is merely a restatement of what he believes is the function of morality.

In that context, the justification Perry gives for his "first principle" takes on considerable significance. It is such a key

---

[8]*Realms of Value,* p. 119.
[9]*Ibid.,* pp. 370-371.

element that the basis for it becomes an important test of the merits of his entire theory. He rejects any view that would justify the acceptance of "harmonious happiness" as the basic criterion through intuition, faith, or emotive preference. Among the conditions any such principle must meet, he says, is that it can be adopted by men through choice (by education and persuasion) and that it can be an effective guide to conduct. However, there may be many standards that would meet those tests, so further justification must be given.

Perry then argues that harmonious happiness can be agreed upon both theoretically and practically. Since his supreme standard is applicable to all interests of all people, theoretically it is impersonal and impartial. On the practical level, he says, it will appeal to people, for in encompassing all interests, it takes each person's interests into account to some extent. Further, a successful value theory must be "a system of concepts verified by the data of human life." What makes Perry confident that his supreme principle is so verified, in my opinion, is his insistence that morality consists basically in harmonizing conflicts. He goes on to say that the main claim for his view is that it gives a good account of a widespread, fundamental, and persistent mode of human behavior for which 'moral' is an appropriate name.[10]

For present purposes, a detailed critique of how empirical Perry's proof is does not seem necessary, although I do not find his arguments impressive. The attempt to harmonize interests is a pervasive characteristic of human behavior, but whether it is as pervasive as Perry thinks is another question. Perhaps some other even more pervasive mode of behavior could be found that would lead to a better value theory. One is tempted to suspect that Perry began with an implicit notion of the good life in terms of harmonious happiness, and then fit as many observable events as he could into that framework, rather than ascertaining through empirical inquiry that humans are disposed to act in conformity with his first principle.

10*Ibid.,* pp. 123-136.

C. PERRY ON VALUE MEASUREMENT

Perry sees as the practical problem of everyday life not the finding of what is good, but the choosing of certain goods from a host of competing goods. The difficulty in grading values lies not in their immeasurability or incommensurability, he says, but in their commensurability. There are a great many sensible ways in which one can speak of more or less of an interest and hence of more or less of a value. When we raise the question of what it is about an object that makes it better or worse than another, we are raising a question that in some sense is quantitative. Perry is quite hard on those who insist on the nonquantitative character of values and who criticize Bentham's quantitative hedonic calculus on the ground that he neglected the difference between "higher" and "lower" values. Such critics are using terms that "are not less quantitative than Bentham's, but only less precise."

Perry also notes that 'quantitative,' 'measurable,' and related terms may be used in restricted senses in the physical sciences, and he does not insist that values are quantitatively measurable in just those senses. He says that it is optional whether we widen those restricted senses so that values are included, or develop some new terminology. But, at least in a broad sense, he clearly finds values measurable. He also differentiates carefully between theoretical and practical impediments to measurements, and does not minimize the difficulties in the way of achieving satisfactory measurements.[11]

In *General Theory of Value*, Perry discusses three independent quantitative criteria for the comparative assessment of values: *intensity, preference,* and *inclusiveness.* These "quantitative principles" correspond closely to what W. E. Johnson and others have labeled "intensive," "distensive," and "extensive" magnitudes. Other things being equal, X is more valuable than Y: (1) if the interest in X is more intense than the interest in Y; (2) or if X is preferred to Y; (3) or if the interest in X is more inclusive than the interest in Y. Perry insists that all three criteria are important and opposes value theories that emphasize only

----

[11]*Realms of Value,* pp. 50-53; *General Theory of Value,* p. 599, p. 608.

preferences. The "order of preference" is different from "the scale of intensities," for they often vary independently. A given person may prefer wine to cold water, and cold water to tepid water, and maintain that preference order while his interest in tepid water, say, undergoes many different degrees of intensity.

Inclusiveness is illustrated in situations in which there is more than one independent interest in the same object. A book valued for its intellectual content and its excellence of manufacture is more valuable than if it were valued for only one of those reasons, other things being equal. Perry says that water desired both for drinking and for bathing is better than water desired for only one of those purposes, "not in the sense of being preferred, nor in the sense of being more intensely desired, but in the sense of being more inclusively desired."

Perry puts strong emphasis on the "superimposition and overlapping" of interests. That often occurs when there are independent interests in the *same* object, but he also holds that inclusiveness is involved when multiple interests have *different* objects. If James has a positive interest in pushpin and John has a positive interest in poetry, there is more value in the combination than in pushpin or poetry singly. Perry goes on to say:

"The standard of inclusiveness, finally, is relative neither to interests nor to objects, but may be applied absolutely. . . . [Inclusiveness] makes possible the comparison of the objects of one interest with the objects of another without the introduction of a third interest, and is therefore the only standard by which all interests can be brought into one system having a maximum in all three respects, or on the whole."[12]

In *Realms of Value*, Perry takes a similar, although somewhat broader and more flexible, approach. He discusses preference, intensity, strength, duration, number, enlightenment, and inclusiveness.

The order of *preference* is characterized as quantitative in

[12]*General Theory of Value*, pp. 615-658; the long quotation is from p. 658. For W. E. Johnson's account of different kinds of magnitude, see his *Logic*, Part II, Cambridge, At the University Press, 1922, Ch. VII.

the sense of being representable "by a line with different stretches or intervals lying between the object which is preferred to all the others (maximum), and the term to which all the others are preferred (minimum)." He objects to prominent value theories that adopt only the preferential standard, not only because he regards that as too narrow, but because such views often lead to the conclusion that values are not measurable at all, or that they can only be measured "intensively" and not "extensively," or to the view that all judgments of comparative value are relative to the person making the judgment.

His treatment of *intensity* is much the same as in his earlier book. He suggests that if pleasantness and unpleasantness are taken as referring to "internal awareness of positive and negative interests, then the relative felt intensities of feeling reflect the relative intensities of the interests themselves," and constitute a serial magnitude. Perry distinguishes *intensity* from *strength*. He holds that an individual, in a given time period, has "a certain fund of available energy, for which his several interests compete." When any one interest "appropriates" some of that fund, the available supply for other interests diminishes. "The strength of an interest, then, is its precedence in this rivalry." He argues that the scale of strength, so understood, is relative to a single organism. Although he does not want to say that one organism's *interest* is stronger than another organism's, we can say, for example, that hunger and sex tend to be among the stronger interests for our species. We also can say that one organism's *appetite* for some object is stronger than another's if that appetite ranks higher in the rivalry for the first organism's total energy fund than it does for the second organism.

According to Perry, *duration* and *number* are standards of comparison that can be applied to any two interests. Interests can be compared in terms of their frequency of manifestation, and one interest can last longer than another. He is careful to point out that a greater duration of an interest does not necessarily imply a greater value in its object: "A long life is better than a short one only provided there is a continuing love of life." Duration can be a standard of value in the sense that "lasting and multiplying positive interests" are thereby facilitated. This should not be confused when a celebration of protracted pursuits *per se,* for great frustration may occur when enjoyments are too long postponed. Numerical comparisons of interests also should not be confused with other comparisons. Simply because four interests are greater than three interests numerically does not imply that they are greater in all respects, or overall. "The numerical comparison leaves other standards of comparison indeterminate, and therefore proves nothing as to the total magnitudes of interest."

Enlightenment is related to what Perry called *correctness* in his earlier book. The optimum interest, judged by the standard of enlightenment, "would be an interest purged of error, and knowing truly whatever was relevant." He warns of confusion between what constitutes an interest and the warrant for statements that may be relevant to the generation of that interest: "An interest whose cognitive mediation is erroneous is nonetheless 'truly' an interest; and though its object's good or evil is founded on error, it is not erroneous to judge its object to be good or evil."

As a preliminary to his discussion of *inclusiveness,* Perry discusses the problem of the overall magnitude of an interest. He mentions that the various magnitudes of an interest could be multiplied together, and that the product could be compared with the similar product for some other interest. But except in special cases, there would be an arbitrary aspect to such a procedure. He says:

> "Unless the factors are themselves commensurable, *inter se,* the amounts assigned to them are quite arbitrary. Where, as in the case of awarding total merit, 'points' are assigned, the weighting of the points is either arbitrary, or is determined by some external principle — such as commercial, athletic, or scholastic standards. The magnitudes of value enumerated above — preference, intensity, strength, duration, number, and enlightenment — are incommensurable, or commensurable within a certain range, or in a certain respect. The quantity obtained by multiplying them together would not describe a total value un-

less they were 'weighted.' The amount of intensity to be equated with an amount of enlightenment or duration, would be entirely arbitrary, or it would reflect some interest imported from outside and introducing a new dimension of value."[13]

He goes on to say that regardless of the type of incommensurability just mentioned, *inclusiveness* is a standard by means of which one aggregate of interests can be compared with another, or with a single interest: "A totality of interests is greater than any of its parts in all respects; that is *whatever* the magnitudes of preference, intensity, strength, or duration, number or enlightenment." So again inclusiveness plays an important role, and helps lead to the first principle of harmonious happiness.

D. CRITICISM OF PERRY

Although Perry does not explore technical questions of scaling in any detail, I think we can agree that in principle interests are measurable along the lines he suggests. He has given a good general account of the various ways interests can vary and be compared. Within that framework, several possible difficulties may be mentioned.

First, although it is clear that Perry intends his theory to be empirical, it is sometimes far from clear just what the specific behavior is that Perry refers to. For example, without having a clear notion of what behavior 'intensity' refers to, we cannot proceed very far in discussing the techniques by which it can be measured. As I see the matter, in principle a view like Perry's can overcome such difficulties, but Perry retained enough of an introspective, nonbehavioral approach to generate some problems.

Second, as Perry himself emphasizes, a comparative measurement of interests is often possible in respect to any one criterion, but an overall assessment requires a weighting of the criteria, and this is difficult to do without being arbitrary or without introducing an additional interest. If we are generously inclined toward Perry, then, we can say that interests are measurable in a

---

[13]*Realms of Value*, pp. 53-61; the long quotation is from p. 60.

great many ways, but how to combine those ways into a single measure without being arbitrary is a serious problem for his theory.

Perhaps even more than Perry himself believed, I think that this latter type of difficulty may be overcome *in theory* by the introduction of the first principle of harmonious happiness. The weighting of the various aspects of interests that is most conducive to harmonious happiness would yield an overall measure of a value. Even so, however, *in practice* we are very far from being able to make the appropriate measurements and weight them properly.

Third, running throughout his value theory is a kind of tension between the "subjective" and the "objective," and between the "individual" and the "social." As noted, some critics mistakenly focus only on the "subjective" and "individual" aspects of Perry's theory, and I do not want to repeat their errors. Rather, I am suggesting that if one begins with simple interests all on a par, and as highly relative to the individual concerned, it is quite difficult and cumbersome to move to a position in which those interests can be judged as "objectively" good or bad and as socially desirable or detrimental. In short, Perry is handicapped by an individual relativism that is difficult to reconcile with social harmonious happiness. (And, as noted, the empirical support for the norm of harmonious happiness is weak.)

In other respects, of course, objectivity is insured in Perry's theory. Whether or not a given individual has an interest of a certain intensity, for example, is objectively ascertainable in principle, and given a certain preference order, some interests should be subordinated to others. But to compare competing preference orders, etc., is difficult on Perry's theory, although I have suggested that least *in theory* harmonious happiness may do that job. As long as one makes values fundamentally dependent on interests, however, and takes as flexible a view of interests as Perry does, some degree of individual relativism seems inescapable. He also has a tendency to make certain inner aspects of behavior, which are difficult to measure, the ultimate determinants of value.

If there were overwhelming evidence in favor of adopting an interest approach to value, the difficulties of measurement flowing from that approach would have to be accepted. If, on the other hand, the evidence does not so favor the interest theory, its difficulties in regard to measurement suggest the wisdom of trying another approach.

E.   PEPPER'S SELECTIVE SYSTEMS

In a sense, Pepper continues in the tradition of Perry's value theory. Pepper focuses attention on the behavior involved in human valuations, and he puts far less emphasis on the language of value discourse than many contemporary philosophers do. His strong effort to see human behavior in evolutionary perspective also differentiates his approach from that of many recent philosophers. In developing his value theory, he pays detailed attention to the work done by psychologists, and also introduces considerable material from other behavioral sciences. Pepper places strong stress on eschewing finality; he regards all of his statements as tentative, hypothetical, and subject to future modification and correction in the light of the evidence.

Pepper's general method can be roughly described as follows: He begins by provisionally accepting ordinary or commonsense views about the boundaries of the value field, but that is only a starting point. Ordinary language, for example, is not a final or even major test of the correctness of a value theory. Once a field of inquiry has been settled on, detailed empirical inquiry is necessary into the behavior occurring in that field. In the process of our inquiry, we may have to make important changes in how we construe that field and its limits, and we may find that many of our cherished views, even though hallowed by long tradition, need serious modification. Both the terminology adopted, and the conclusions reached, are to be tested by the empirical evidence; we do not begin with either fixed terminology or with incorrigible principles, facts, or presuppositions.

More technically, Pepper emphasizes what he calls a "descriptive definition." In empirical inquiry, he says:

". . . the constructive employment of a definition . . . is to set the initial bounds and target for the subject matter to be investigated, and then to summarize the results of the inquiry in its terminal stages. The successive refinements of the initial definition . . . mark the progress of the inquiry. The definitions formulated in the course of such an inquiry are all supposed to be true to the facts investigated. It is their conformity to the facts that controls their successive refinements and dictates the acceptance or rejection of a definition in the progress of the inquiry."[14]

Pepper views purposive behavior as a type of adaptive behavior. Adaptive behavior has two main subdivisions: automatic reflex behavior and docile behavior. Docile behavior is modifiable by learning, as automatic reflex behavior is not; the behavior necessary to obtain an object (or avoid it) must be acquired or learned. Roughly, 'purposive behavior' is 'docile adaptive behavior.' A positive purposive act (appetition) has a twofold goal: a goal object and a quiescence pattern. Negative purposive acts (aversions) cannot be reduced to appetitions, nor is their structure the same. There is, then, what Pepper calls a "molar opposition" between appetition and aversion within purposive behavior.

In addition, there are "three selective polarities": conation (favoring or liking as opposed to disfavoring or disliking); affection (pleasure as opposed to pain); and achievement (success as opposed to frustration). All are involved in purposive behavior. Pepper thinks many other value theorists mistakenly emphasize only one of the three; for example, Perry put too much emphasis on conation. In much the same fashion that Perry criticized those who focus only on one of the standards through which comparative value can be assessed (such as preference), Pepper argues that many proposed views are too narrow and that his broader view of purposive value better fits the empirical data.[15]

'Selective system' is a crucial term in Pepper's theory. He

[14]Stephen C. Pepper, *The Sources of Value,* Berkeley, University of California Press, 1958, Introduction, Chs. 1, 13, 21. The long quotation is from p. 282.
[15]*Ibid.,* Chs. 2 and 14.

suggests that this notion has implicitly guided empirical moralists throughout the history of ethical theory, and in his own theory it links together "successive levels of value." Indeed, he takes 'selective system' as "the defining concept for the term 'value' as this is traced out in the present study." 'Value,' then, is identified with selective systems among docile organisms. A selective system is a dynamic structure operating to eliminate errors and accumulate correct results; criteria for correctness are generated, and errors are corrected, by means of the same dynamics.

Let us look at two examples that help to illustrate what Pepper has in mind. In carpentry, the goal may be to build a house, construct some cupboards, etc., and numerous subordinate activities such as sawing, planing, and hammering are involved. Many mistakes or errors can occur, such as making joints of insufficient strength or taking an inefficient and roundabout way of achieving the goal. The activity or process of carpentry thus generates various standards, and learning frequently helps the carpenter to move from a bad performance to a highly skilled performance. As the process develops temporally, there is a marked tendency to eliminate errors and reinforce skilled performances. Another type of example mentioned concerns a common social situation; a son wants the family car to take his girl to a game. Many factors may be involved in coming to the final decision, such as the condition of the car, the driving ability of the son, and the length of time since he last had the car. Pepper argues that in principle there is a best solution for such a situation and that the structure of the particular situation is the criterion for the correctness of the solution. If a poor decision results, when a similar situation arises in the future the earlier decision can be taken into account, and in this sense a "natural norm" is generated.[16]

In accord with his principle of the progressive refinement of key notions on the basis of ongoing empirical inquiry, Pepper finally arrives at this account of 'selective system':

---

[16]*Ibid.*, p. 3, pp. 524-526; also, Stephen C. Pepper, *A Digest of Purposive Values*, Berkeley, University of California Press, 1947, pp. 81-82.

> *"A selective system is a structural process by which a unitary dynamic agency is channeled in such a way that it generates particular acts, dispositions, or objects (to be called 'trials'), and also activates a specific selective agency (to be called 'the norm') by which some of the trials are rejected and others are incorporated into the dynamic operation of the system."*[17]

A selective system is differentiated from other modes of selection because it has what Pepper calls a "split dynamics." The same dynamics that generate the norm also generate the trials which are selected pro and con. To illustrate, he contrasts a selective system to a sieve. Even though a sieve separates larger from smaller particles, neither group is correct or incorrect with respect to the structure of the sieve or to each other. The sieve, then, is not "normative" with respect to either size particle; in contrast, a selective system itself institutes both norms and trials, all with the same dynamics. These dynamics result from purposive drives or from evolutionary selection.

Pepper finds seven main selective systems, which he analyzes in great detail: purposive acts, consummatory fields, personal situations, personality structures, social situations, cultural patterns, and natural selection. Each of these generates specific norms or selective agencies through which particular acts, dispositions, or objects are accepted or rejected. Pepper feels that these seven systems *in toto* cover what is commonly regarded as the value field, although it must be remembered that common sense is merely a rough guide to the field of behavior involved, not the main test of what is acceptable.

As the final element of Pepper's theory to be mentioned here, let us look briefly at each of the seven selective systems to see what the characteristic types of norms, trials, and values are.

In *purposive acts,* conative-achievement values are generated. The norm is the reduction of a drive, and the trials are the subordinate acts engaged in. In *consummatory fields,* "gratuitous satisfactions" are involved. These are patterns of neuromuscular tensions that are not strong enough to require trial-and-error behavior to reduce the tension, but yet yield satisfaction under

---

[17]*The Sources of Value,* pp. 667-668.

proper circumstances; for example, we sometimes eat just to enjoy a taste even when our hunger drive has already been satisfied. The norm in this selective system is the maximizing of the gratuitous satisfactions available, and the trials consist in the acts of locating the optimum conditions for satisfaction. The values are affective values.

In *personal situations,* prudential values are generated. The norm is the maximum of achievement and of gratuitous satisfaction available from the contributory drives, and the trials are the organism's resultant acts. In *personality structures,* character values are generated. Two types of norm are found: personality roles demanding conformity, such as conscience, and norms of personality integration. The acts of a person constitute the trials for the first type, and personality dispositions make up the trials for the second norm.

In *social situations,* the values generated are social values. The norm is the maximum reduction of tension or the development of consummatory satisfactions for all the people involved. The trials are the resultant acts that are performed. In *cultural patterns,* cultural values are generated through two types of norm: institutions demanding conformity, and cultural integration. For the first type of norm, the trials are social acts that occur in a social situation involving a cultural institution. For the second type, the trials are the institutions themselves.

In *natural selection,* survival values are generated. The norm is the continuance of an interbreeding population (including the development of new species adapted to a new life zone). In natural selection in general, individual offspring constitute the trials; in highly socialized species, the trials are societies of organisms; and for man, the trials are mainly cultural patterns.

As has been noted, in each system natural norms are generated, and some of the trials are favorably selected while others tend to be eliminated. To give one final illustration, for *cultural patterns,* individuals who do not conform to cultural institutions tend to be punished in one way or another, and institutions showing a marked cultural lag tend to be modified.[18] Pepper's account

---

18*Ibid.,* pp. 662-673.

of each selective system is elaborate and detailed, and he relies heavily on the relevant work of behavioral scientists. Any brief summary of Pepper's account, such as that given here, may tend to make his work seem either less clear or more dogmatic than it is. However, for present purposes I believe enough has been said to set the stage for a discussion of Pepper's views on value measurement.

F. PEPPER ON VALUE MEASUREMENT

Like Perry, Pepper does not attempt to develop any particular scale or set of scales for measuring values, but he discusses the respects in which values are measurable quantitatively. He agrees with Perry that at least some writers who abhor viewing values as quantitative in fact have developed theories that involve a quantitative dimension for values. Just as in hedonistic theories the more pleasure, the better, and the more pain, the worse, so theories defining 'good' in terms of union with God and 'evil' in terms of a fall from God imply that the nearer God, the better, and the further away, the worse. Any relation expressible in terms of more or less is a quantitative relation, according to Pepper.

Pepper also emphasizes an obvious but often neglected point: that what is or is not quantitative about values depends on the view of value adopted. For example, George Santayana took 'aesthetic value' as 'objectified pleasure' in his *Sense of Beauty*. On his view, although pleasure is quantifiable, objectification apparently is not. Pleasure either is or is not objectified; no degrees of objectification are possible. And sometimes values are so construed that they are in principle incapable of quantification. Benedetto Croce, for example, defined the field of aesthetics in terms of intuition, and viewed each occurrence of an aesthetic intuition as an immediate and unique qualitative experience. Whether or not the aesthetic spectator has such an intuition can be determined, but not how much of an intuition it is. As a final illustration, for typical hedonistic views pleasures and pains are directly quantifiable in terms of intensity, duration, and number.

Pepper further points out that given a demarcated value field, all sorts of quantitative criteria can be applied; the problem is to ascertain which ones are relevant. He distinguishes between intrinsic and extrinsic standards, with the former being the basically relevant standards. Such intrinsic standards "consist in the quantification of the defining characters of the definitional criterion of value." Thus for Perry, generic value is measured in terms of those aspects of an interest that are quantifiable; on some other theory, different standards would be intrinsic. (Pepper adds a qualification. For a given value theory there may be characters of values that could serve as "defining characters" but are not included in the definition because they are unnecessary for practical identification. Such characters may also be quantifiable and sources of intrinsic standards.)

An extrinsic standard is some feature of the situation "that is more or less reliably correlated with the intrinsic characters of the definition," although not itself a defining feature. For example, in some value theories health would be a relevant extrinsic standard, since it correlates highly with the capacity to realize values. If there is no correlation, the standard under consideration is irrelevant. Extrinsic standards, then, represent intrinsic standards, and often are easier to apply operationally.

This brings us back to Pepper's discussion of "descriptive definition"; we need to keep in mind not only the extent to which a given definition of 'value' allows quantification, but how adequate such a definition is for the field we are attempting to describe. In inquiry into the empirical connections of a particular value field, during which we improve and refine our application of the term 'value,' we may find that what we initially took as intrinsic is not intrinsic, and we may also discover intrinsic standards that we did not initially suspect were involved.

As does Perry, Pepper differentiates three types of quantitative relations: the extensive, the intensive, and the distensive.

Extensive measurement is based on the relation of a whole to its parts. The parts may or may not be divisible into smaller parts of the same kind. In length, for example, whatever length is adopted as the unit of measurement is itself divisible into smaller lengths of the same kind. In other cases, such as that of human populations, the persons comprising a population are not themselves divisible into smaller persons. Pepper goes on to say that sometimes the parts "can be intuitively apprehended in the whole" (as in a bag of marbles), but in other instances the whole may be too large for such apprehension. And often we are interested in greater accuracy than "intuition" allows. Measurement is called for both when we want accuracy and when an intuitive apprehension is not possible.

In intensive measurement, Pepper says, it is not possible to perceive separate units within the whole; a loud sound is not "intuited" as composed of many soft sounds. Yet for a given pitch, a loud sound is perceived as a greater sound than a soft sound, and thus for Pepper is a quantitative difference. Usually in intensive measurement some method of correlating degrees of intensity with degrees of extensity is used, as when intensities of sound are correlated with the energies of air vibration, which in turn are correlated with pointer readings on some measuring device. But Pepper insists the intuitive differences are basic, and the significance of the pointer readings depends on them. He says:

> "The correlation of intensities of sound with the energy of air waves registered on a chart is simply an ingenious device for giving greater accuracy and permanence to measurements of the intensity of sound. The direct intuitive measurements of intensity are not reduced away by the device; they are still essential to the significance of the correlation."

He adds that most quantitative value judgments have to be made by direct intuitive measurement, for there are few devices for correlating our intuitions with pointer readings on scales. For the near future, at least, a precise quantitative measurement of values is not to be expected.

Distensive measurement involves the determination of the degree of difference between two things, such as in musical pitches or color hues. Often these distensive quantities can be arrayed in order of increasing difference from some point adopted as the origin, as in an array of just noticeable differences in psychophysics. In value fields, distensive quantity is illustrated by how close or far something is from an ideal.

Pepper, again in the spirit of Perry, argues that often it is extremely important to distinguish these three types of quantity, for to get the greatest overall quantity of value it may be important to weight some of the quantities, and maximizing one may tend to diminish the others. Taking account of all three is important for the overall field of value.

In terms of maximizing human values, Pepper returns to his distinction between survival values and affective values. When survival values are at stake, their dynamics tend to take precedence over those of affective values. Humans have learned that maximizing happiness requires that survival needs be met.

> "The strategy for man, who can to a considerable degree control situations, is hereby laid out with realistic clarity. Constituted as he is, a docile animal endowed through his inherited repertory of drives with a capacity for happiness (for maximizing pleasures as well as minimizing pains), he *naturally* (in the literal sense of the term) has a bias for maximizing affection and satisfying his own basic drives. But he can achieve much happiness for himself only if he can keep the pressures from survival values at a distance."

Historically, two different strategies have been used to increase an individual's satisfactions and keep survival pressures at a distance. The first is that of personally withdrawing from the world as much as possible, and accommodating oneself to satisfactions that can be gained with a minimal involvement in social institutions. Such an escape method works after a fashion, and in times of desperate social conditions may even be the best path for some individuals to follow. The other path is through social control, in the sense of using intelligent foresight to develop well-adapted social structures that afford a high degree of survival values and free individuals to develop their individual satisfactions. In short, the maximizing of individual values requires an appropriate social setting.[19]

G. CRITICISM OF PEPPER

Throughout this book I have followed the practice of adhering closely to the terminology of the various authors considered, even when I thought a revised terminology would be an improvement. Partly I adopted that practice because terminological differences can reflect substantive differences, and a translation into different terminology might distort the view under discussion. In addition, the terminological problems in value inquiry are great, and to exhibit some of the differences and difficulties as we go along may be useful.

Although I am in agreement with at least the main drift of what Pepper says, I think that his terminology sometimes may suggest views that he rejects. For example, his emphasis on "intuition" in the discussion of measurement strikes me as possibly misleading, and in at least some instances it seems clear enough that all he has in mind is the perceivings of individuals under certain specifiable circumstances. Neglecting these terminological differences, in my opinion Pepper has discussed many significant problems of value measurement, and his emphasis on the behavior involved in valuating eliminates many of the problems about the peculiarly "inner" experiences that are often postulated in value theories.

I also agree with the elementary but strangely neglected point that rushing headlong into questions about the measurement of value without first giving great care to how the term 'value' is applied is wasteful and often productive of marked confusion.

Although I agree with Pepper that in general we are far from having satisfactory scales for measuring various aspects of values, I am less pessimistic than he is about the theoretical possibility of developing such scales. In my view, at least, the problem may

---

[19]*Ibid.*, pp. 288-302, pp. 679-682. The two long quotations are from p. 295 and p. 679.

be less the intrinsic difficulties in working up usable scales than
that such an approach is anathema to so many people. If a sufficient number of workers could come to at least general agreement about what behavior they were referring to when they
talked about values, and then turned their attention to developing appropriate scales, the results might be better and arrived at
sooner than Pepper suggests.

Possibly the greatest problem in Pepper's value theory as
developed to date concerns the maximizing of value. Although
much that he says on the negative side about practical difficulties
is well taken, I do not find a clear and convincing account of how
theoretically values may be maximized. Granted that a basic
practical problem is finding modes of social organization so that
survival problems are not pressing, just how do we balance the
"demands" of the various selective systems? I think Pepper has
described well the role of cultural institutions play in "forcing"
conformity from individuals, and what he says about cultural
lag has its point. But suppose a given individual concludes on
the evidence that a given "powerful" cultural institution operates
so as to impede, hinder, or diminish the realization of important
values. To illustrate, many instances can be found in which there
was great cultural opposition to new and significant developments
in medical science. Given a certain type of cultural organization,
in the long run such opposition may disappear, but in the shorter
run, how do we balance such competing items? Fighting too hard
in favor of some new medical development may endanger the
survival of an individual, not to mention the maximizing of his
affective values, but failing to fight may imperil other values.

At this point, I want to emphasize that many value theories
develop some such difficulty in one way or another and a frequently chosen "way out" is to so oversimplify the behavioral
situation that some of the important complexities are eliminated
by fiat. So, although I think Pepper's view generates the kind of
difficulty I have just discussed, he deserves considerable credit
for not oversimplifying matters.

In summary, I think Pepper has, in his account of the seven
selective systems, encompassed most of the behavior that we

would be tempted to label value behavior. He also has discussed in an impressive way some of the general problems of value measurement as values are construed in his theory, and he has indicated something about the types of scale that would be appropriate for actual measurement. On the other hand, at least on my reading of his work, he is left with some difficult problems of how to maximize values overall, and he has been perhaps too skeptical about the possibility of developing precise measurements.

H.   CONCLUSION

As would be expected, behavioral scientists writing on value measurement are likely to put most of their emphasis on the development of appropriate scales, while philosophers are more likely to emphasize what they see as the most defensible uses of value terms. At this point, we should note that whatever else might be said in favor of typical behavioral science attempts to develop scales for value measurement, those attempts usually involve only one part of what Pepper and Perry talk about. The apparent technical neatness of some scientific metrics, then, should always be judged against the range of behavior involved. Many scales concern only one aspect of what is often taken as the value field; such a restriction of ordinary attitudes may turn out to be evidentially justifiable, but at times what happens is that such a restricted behavioral field (e.g., preferences) is confused with a much more inclusive one.

Although both Perry and Pepper take a fundamentally empirical approach to values, in some respects the influence of nonempirical historical views seems noticeable; especially traces of the view that in the value field we are concerned primarily with "inner" processes. Thus both Perry and Pepper put considerable emphasis on the way certain phenomena are perceived by the individuals involved, and note how difficult it may be to develop an "objective" quantified measure of such things. I think both authors make too much of problems such as the felt or perceived intensity involved in valuational behavior.

If we take as a major goal (as Pepper does) the prediction of the relevant human behavior, the felt intensity and in general the phenomena as perceived by an individual may not have as much importance as sometimes is assumed. For example, we might be able to predict quite well the behavior of a starving man without finding it necessary to measure the "subjective" strength of his feeling of acute hunger.

Often the type of problem under discussion is analyzed in terms of the correlation of "subjective" events with "objective" events. For example, without the aid of measuring devices, we may make certain judgments of the length of a line, and the behavior involved can then be compared to the results of a measurement of that line according to some standard set of procedures. Rather than stress the correlation of the "subjective" with the "objective," I think we would do better to pose inquiry in terms of two different types of behavior. It may be worth-while to compare those two types; in some instances we may want to study only the first type and in other instances only the second type.

When we come to preferences, at least sometimes finding out the objective result of measurement may affect the preference. If two quantities of gold, intuitively compared, seem to be the same, an individual may be indifferent as to which he would choose. But if he were informed that one quantity weighs more than the other, his indifference may change to a preference for the heavier amount. Or a person who does not initially prefer one dessert to another may develop a strong preference when he finds that one has many more calories than the other. As Pepper emphasizes, often our intuitive estimates are intertwined with other aspects of behavior in significant ways, and finding a method of correlating intuitive differences with reliable "pointer readings" may be useful. But if the pointer reading measurements are highly useful in predicting behavior that we want to predict, their correlation with our intuitions may not be of particular importance.

In somewhat different ways, both Pepper and Perry seem to have some difficulty in linking the "individual" and the "social."

Both theories seem most adequate when the standpoint of one individual only is considered; the problem of maximizing the values for one individual seems more adequately handled than that of maximizing values for groups. Perry approaches group maximization issues through the introduction of his first principle of harmonious happiness, and Pepper discusses in some detail not only survival values but the sociocultural setting in which humans behave. But their ways of linking together individuals and social groups tend to have less empirical support than other aspects of their theories, and it is sometimes difficult to see what criteria apply in maximizing social values.

Although the matter is complicated, I suggest that the root difficulty may lie in beginning with individuals separated too much from their sociocultural settings. If, instead, from the beginning we emphasize the biosocial nature of mankind, and refuse to separate radically the "individual" and the "social," I believe many of those problems would be by-passed. Some of these issues will be discussed in the next chapter.[20]

---

[20]I have considered the value theories of Perry and Pepper much more fully, and compared their work to other approaches, in my *Value Theory and the Behavioral Sciences*, Springfield, Charles C Thomas, 1969. My account in this chapter is based on that book.

Chapter VIII

VALUES AS PREFERENCES AND AS NEED SATISFACTIONS

A. PURPOSE OF CHAPTER

In the last chapter, an interest theory of value was compared to a view emphasizing selective systems. In this chapter, a theory making preferences basic to value will be compared to one that takes need satisfactions as basic. All four theories are "naturalistic" and show sympathy for a scientific approach to value. As part of my overall thesis, I have maintained that 'value' is used in enough different and conflicting ways so that an important problem is selecting the most appropriate use for that term. If one is committed to the merits of scientific inquiry into values, one criterion in selecting among alternative proposed uses of 'value' is the degree to which scientific inquiry is facilitated. In judging the degree of facilitation, the consequences for measurement of adopting a proposed use of 'value' is a factor to be taken into account.

As we have seen, many writers emphasize the role of preferences in value theory. The work of Charles Morris will be given particular attention in this chapter, for he has not only discussed value theory in considerable detail, he has also conducted an extensive empirical inquiry into values. As a contrast to Morris' theoretical orientation, my own need theory of value will also be considered.[1]

---

[1]The main material used here comes from two of Morris' books: *Varieties of Human*

B. MORRIS[1] GENERAL POINT OF VIEW

Morris says that he was strongly influenced by American pragmatists, such as Charles Peirce, William James, and John Dewey, who believed that evaluations were much like scientific judgments and that a scientific approach to values was both possible and would be useful to man as a valuer. Morris sees his inquiry into value behavior as a "serious empirical test" of those views.[2]

Morris emphasizes the term 'preferential behavior.' That behavior is called positive if an organism acts in such a way as either to maintain the presence of an object or situation, or to construct that object or situation if it is not present. Negative preferential behavior is exhibited if the organism strives to move away from, destroy, or prevent the object or situation. In principle, he says, such behavior can be studied scientifically. He further takes 'value situation' as any situation involving preferential behavior. A value situation is "inherently relational," for it involves a response to something. A pain *per se* is not a value, but is a value if responded to by negative (or positive) preferential behavior. He goes on to say that he takes values as "objectively relative," since they are properties relative to preferential behavior; a value does not exist in and of itself.[3] (Morris' approach here has similarities to what is called transactionalism in this book.)

If one focuses on what Morris calls the whole value situation (transaction), he says it becomes understandable "why the term 'value' is so vague — in different contexts it is used to signify different aspects of value situations." Three of those usages have special importance.

(1) Operative Values. Often 'value' is used to "refer to the tendencies or dispositions of living beings to prefer one kind of object rather than another." If, for example, a person is shown

---

Value, Chicago, University of Chicago Press, 1956, and *Signification and Significance: A Study of the Relations of Signs and Values,* Cambridge, M. I. T. Press, 1964. The need theory discussed here is developed in my *Value Theory and the Behavioral Sciences,* Springfield, Charles C Thomas, 1969, especially Ch. VII.

[2]Morris, *Varieties of Human Value,* p. vii.

[3]Morris, *Signification and Significance,* pp. 16-19.

pairs of paintings (one a landscape and the other a portrait), and always or usually chooses the portrait, "we can say that his operative value is for portrayals of persons rather than landscapes." 'Operative value,' then, "signifies the direction of preferential behavior of a given individual in a variety of situations."

(2) *Conceived Values.* Sometimes 'value' is used to refer to behavior that is guided by anticipation or foresight of the outcome. The example Morris gives is of a drug addict who firmly believes it is preferable not to be addicted; he anticipates what the outcome would be of not using drugs, approves that state, and regards it as preferable. A conceived value, then, involves a preference for symbolically indicated objects; or to use the technical language of Morris' later book: "Some object or situation is signified and liked or disliked as signified." On Morris' view, then, a conceived value necessarily involves signs, but operative values may or may not. He argues that both for individuals and groups there is always some divergence between operative and conceived values.

(3) *Object Values.* In his earlier book, Morris discusses this use of 'value' in the context of what is preferable or desirable, whether or not it is actually preferred or conceived as preferable. His example is that of a diabetic who seeks advice from a dietitian as to the preferable diet for one with that illness. The diabetic may himself have a conception of the appropriate diet, but his conception can be mistaken. For that matter, the dietitian's conception can also be mistaken. "Value here is not characterized in terms of what is in fact preferred but in terms of what in fact is preferable if the patient prefers to live rather than to die." In his later book, Morris gives a somewhat different account:

> "Some objects (or situations) are such that they support (or would support) positive preferential behavior to them by some organisms. Others are such that contact with them leads to (or would lead to) negative preferential behavior by some organisms. Thus, as I have already argued, object values are objectively relative; i.e., they are properties of an object considered in relation to its ability to reinforce preferential behavior directed toward it by some organisms."

Although the modification of Morris' earlier views raises some interesting topics, we need not go into them here since they are not important for Morris' empirical work on values as described in his earlier book. In that book, he emphasizes that all three uses of 'value' can be explicated with respect to some form of 'prefer.' Value may be taken as the preferred, or as a conception of the preferable, or as what is actually preferable. He goes on:

> "The main contrast is between preferred and preferable (desired and desirable, valued and valuable, esteemed and estimable). What is preferred (operative values) can be found through a study of preferential behavior. What is conceived to be preferable (conceived values) can be studied through the symbols employed in preferential behavior and the preferential behavior directed toward symbols."[4]

Despite Morris' insistence that values are objectively relative and thus involve both subjects and objects, his account of the three types of values seems to oscillate between locating the value in the person and in the object. He sometimes contrasts the preferred to the preferable, which seems to make the value an object, or property, or situation, etc. Yet at other times, he takes an operative value as a *tendency or disposition* to prefer one object rather than another, which seems to locate value within the person. Such oscillation is often found; it was discussed earlier in relation to Clark Hull's work (Chapter III), and also in relation to transactionalism as opposed to interactionism.

As we shall see, this generates some difficulty when values are measured by Morris' techniques. To illustrate one such difficulty, suppose a given person prefers an apple to an orange. If we call the apple the value, we are measuring one kind of thing; if we call the person's tendency to prefer apples the value, we are measuring something else; if we shift uncritically between the two uses of 'value,' incoherence may result.

---

[4]Morris' discussion of the three uses of 'value' is on pp. 9-12 of *Varieties of Human Value* and pp. 19-20 of *Signification and Significance.*

C. THE WAYS OF LIFE QUESTIONNAIRE

The main part of Morris' empirical study of values was done with a document called "Ways to Live," responses to which were gained from a large number of college students in various cultures. The "ways to live" are taken by Morris as thirteen conceptions of the good life containing values supported and advocated in mankind's ethical and religious systems. A brief characterization of each Way follows:

Way 1: preserve the best that man has attained
Way 2: cultivate independence of persons and things
Way 3: show sympathetic concern for others
Way 4: experience festivity and solitude in alternation
Way 5: act and enjoy life through group participation
Way 6: constantly master changing conditions
Way 7: integrate action, enjoyment, and contemplation
Way 8: live with wholesome, carefree enjoyment
Way 9: wait in quiet receptivity
Way 10: control the self stoically
Way 11: meditate on the inner life
Way 12: chance adventuresome deeds
Way 13: obey the cosmic purposes.

Initially, the first seven Ways (developed by Morris on the basis of his earlier work) were presented to several hundred college students, who were asked to rate each Way on the basis of how much they liked or disliked it. So many students said that none of those Ways were much to their liking that Morris decided to enlarge the instrument. On the basis both of the students' suggestions and further consideration of historically significant religious and ethical systems, three more Ways were added. When that was done, the respondents' suggestions for additional alternatives decreased. Because of the suggestions that were made and because Morris thought he should include some "obviously extreme alternatives," three further Ways were added, to bring the total to thirteen. This became the basic instrument in Morris' study, and very few plausible new alternatives were suggested when that instrument was used.

To give a fuller notion of the questionnaire, the complete description of the first two Ways is quoted below:

"WAY 1: In this 'design for living' the individual actively participates in the social life of his community, not to change it primarily, but to understand, appreciate, and preserve the best that man has attained. Excessive desires should be avoided and moderation sought. One wants the good things of life but in an orderly way. Life is to have clarity, balance, refinement, control. Vulgarity, great enthusiasm, irrational behavior, impatience, indulgence are to be avoided. Friendship is to be esteemed but not easy intimacy with many people. Life is to have discipline, intelligibility, good manners, predictability. Social changes are to be made slowly and carefully, so that what has been achieved in human culture is not lost. The individual should be active physically and socially, but not in a hectic or radical way. Restraint and intelligence should give order to an active life."

"WAY 2: The individual should for the most part 'go it alone,' assuring himself of privacy in living quarters, having much time to himself, attempting to control his own life. One should stress self-sufficiency, reflection and meditation, knowledge of himself. The direction of interests should be away from intimate associations with social groups, and away from the physical manipulation of objects or attempts at control of the physical environment. One should aim to simplify one's external life, to moderate those desires whose satisfaction is dependent upon physical and social forces outside of oneself, and to concentrate attention upon the refinement, clarification, and self-direction of oneself. Not much can be done or is to be gained by 'living outwardly.' One must avoid dependence upon persons or things; the center of life should be found within oneself."

Each subject was asked to rate each Way using a scale of 1 through 7: 7 indicating that the Way was liked very much, 6 that it was liked quite a lot, 5 that it was liked slightly, 4 that the subject was indifferent, 3 that it was disliked slightly, 2 that it was disliked quite a lot, and 1 that it was disliked very much. The most extensive samples came from the U. S. A., China, and India: some 2015 male college students and 831 female college students from the U. S. completed the questionnaire; 523 men and 220 women from China; and 724 men and 410 women from India. Fairly sizable samples came from Japan, Norway, and Canada, and smaller samples from Pakistan, England, New Zealand, and Italy. The original plan had been to get materials from twenty national groups, but that was not feasible.

In addition to the Ways to Live document, some subjects rated colored reproductions of paintings, and were asked to appraise the paintings as works of art as well as to express their own likes and dislikes. Some subjects were asked to rate the Ways both in terms of how they believed they ought to live and how they in fact lived. About 100 students in each of the main cultures studied (China, India, and the U. S.) were also interviewed as to their main interests, expected careers, etc. A Sheldon somatotype rating was made of those students, tests of temperament were given, etc. Some students were given the Allport-Vernon-Lindzey Study of Values test. Other devices were also used for testing certain subjects.

Morris argues that the ratings on the Ways to Live questionnaire are about conceived values primarily. If the students respond according to the instructions, they are expressing preferences about symbolically formulated alternatives of the good life, and hence about one kind of conceived value. He notes that some critics may see no difference between expressing a preference for, say, food alternatives and for ways of life, and thus conclude that operative values are being investigated. Morris continues:

> "It is, of course, true that one may prefer certain symbol combinations to others just as one prefers certain foods to others. But in the present instance the symbol combinations are themselves formulated approvals of one mode of life rather than another; therefore to like one symbolically formulated alternative more than another is to like one conception of the good life more than another. The ratings may therefore be regarded as indications of conceived values of the respondents."

Without going into this topic in detail, I suggest that the matter may be more complex than Morris indicates. If individuals are asked to express preferences about foods in a questionnaire, those alternatives are also symbolically presented (although of course, they may not be presented in terms of approval for any particular food), and we would not necessarily have measured what actually would be chosen, but what the respondent says he prefers. In any event, the data obtained by Morris consist of respondents' ratings of the degree to which they like or dislike various conceptions of the good life (assuming they have followed instructions).[5]

D. TREATMENT OF THE DATA

Morris discusses the various types of scale that may be possible in measuring the preferences expressed in his data. He found that most subjects ranked the seven rating categories (7 . . . 1) so that they formed an *ordinal* scale (although a few subjects gave 4 as the lowest rating for any of the Ways). Such a rank ordering alone, Morris says, can be useful. However, an *ordinal* scale is not as useful as having an *interval* scale, in which the difference between any two adjacent response categories (e.g., 7 and 6) is the same as that between other adjacent categories (e.g., 3 and 2). Even when the intervals are the same, we may not have a *ratio* scale (one with a nonarbitrary zero point) in which an item given a rating of 6 is liked twice as much as one given a rating of 3.

Extensive statistical treatment[6] was made of the intervals in the data from 250 male U. S. college students. The intervals between the seven response categories turned out not to be equal but to show a lengthening toward the ends of the scale. The numerical results in the data, however, can be corrected so that a given interval "denotes the same psychological 'distance' regardless of its position on the scale." Morris continues:

---

[5]The aspects of Morris' work discussed in this section are from *Varieties of Human Value*, pp. 1-19.

[6]The methods are reported in detail in Charles Morris and Lyle V. Jones, "Value Scales and Dimensions," *Journal of Abnormal and Social Psychology*, Vol. LI, 1955.

176 — The Measurement of Values

"If, then, the original ratings of the Ways were replaced by these corrected numerical values, they could be subjected to all mathematical calculations appropriate to an interval scale. The computing of product-moment correlations, means, and standard deviations is thus justified. In a genuine sense values are then being measured, and the measurements can be made across the cultures from which the scale was derived as well as within the cultures."[7]

Moreover, Morris holds that it is reasonable to assume that the midpoint of Category 4 (indicating indifference) is the zero point of the scale, and says if that assumption is correct, "then the scale is a ratio scale, and measurement of value in the full sense of the term is possible." However, he does not investigate that assumption in any detail.

Morris also points out that methodologically it would be best not to work with the original ratings but to replace them with corrected numerical values on the derived interval scale. But because so much of the calculation had been done before the scaling analysis was made, it was much more convenient not to make that change. So an investigation was made of the difference between using the corrected values and using the original ratings taken *as if* they marked equal scale intervals. For many purposes, Morris says, "the results are practically the same," and so the original (uncorrected) ratings were used for calculating correlations.

E. SOME RESULTS

One problem of interest to Morris was the "isolation of primary dimensions" in the value domain he was investigating. For some purposes each of the thirteen Ways could be taken as a separate dimension, but since some of the Ways had features in common, the finding of a smaller number of primary dimensions might "simplify and clarify the structure of value space." Factor analysis of the data from some U. S. males showed there were five

---

[7]Morris, *Varieties of Human Value*, p. 23. The general material on scaling discussed here is from Ch. 2 of that book.

independent dimensions in the thirteen Ways, and those dimensions were also found reasonably applicable to the Indian and Chinese data. The names Morris gave to those five factors are: Social Restraint and Self-Control, Enjoyment and Progress in Action, Withdrawal and Self-Sufficiency, Receptivity and Sympathetic Concern, and Self-Indulgence or Sensuous Enjoyment. Morris says this conclusion should not be understood as saying that there are only five primary dimensions in the whole value field. He maintains only that factors "of considerable stability" have been found, and that they may be useful in further studies.

Morris describes the three major results of his study as the achieving of a cross-cultural interval scale for measuring values, the isolation of the five value dimensions for his three main national samples, and the amassing of evidence supporting a "field conception of values." In defense of the last point, he says:

"Evidence was given that the ratings of the Ways (and hence the value factor scores) varied with differences in sex, somatotype, temperament, character, intracultural traditions, economic status, and size of community in which the subjects were raised. The methods employed did not permit a precise determination of the relative contributions which the various determinants made to the ratings. It was evident, however, that the differences between the cultures studied tended to be larger than the variations in the above determinants within a culture. As to the intracultural determinants, psychological and constitutional differences seem to play the greatest part in the rating of the Ways, with population variations and economic status next in importance, and with sex and body-size differences playing the smallest part . . . [V]alues, in so far as they are reflected in such ratings, occur in a field and are responsive to many kinds of variation in the field. Hence the scientific study of values ultimately can be carried on only as an interdisciplinary enterprise."[8]

A great number of comparisons are made and specific conclusions are reached in the course of Morris' work. To illustrate, he compares the ratings on the Ways with the results for those

[8]Morris, *Varieties of Human Values*, pp. 32-34, pp. 184-186. The long quotation is from p. 186.

subjects who also took the Allport-Vernon-Lindzey Study of Values test. Although there were some interesting congruences, there also were some marked differences. Morris suggests that this is accounted for because the Allport-Vernon-Lindzey scale measures operative values rather than conceived values and also puts more emphasis on institutionalized social roles than does the Ways to Live instrument.[9]

Later on, Morris and some co-workers gave their questionnaire to 50 noninstitutionalized psychiatric patients, to 50 spouses or closest friends of those patients, and to 50 normal people. One hypothesis was that the more a patient's values diverge from the average values of his culture, the greater the degree of severity of his disturbance. However, this hypothesis was not supported by the data, and deviations of individual values from cultural values "do not in themselves seem to lead to personality disturbances that require psychiatric help."[10] (It is interesting to note that von Mering, using different techniques, came to a similar conclusion. See Chapter V, Section F.)

F.   COMMENTS ON MORRIS

Morris discusses certain limitations which characterize his inquiry. First, the restriction to college students raises questions as to the usefulness of his instrument for noncollege populations. And within the college population, he notes that the total sample may be biased in favor of students from the humanities and the social sciences, including psychology. Second, practical problems of data collection made for a less controlled and systematic approach than was desired. Third, Morris describes the Ways as being primarily "positive in tone, normal rather than abnormal, constructive rather than destructive, beneficent rather than malevolent." He goes on to say that some modes of life are destructive, malevolent, etc., and inquiry into those modes is im-

---

[9]*Ibid.*, pp. 109-111.

[10]Morris, *Signification and Significance*, pp. 85-86. The study is given in more detail in Charles Morris, Bernice T. Eiduson, and Dennis O'Donovan, "Values of Psychiatric Patients," *Behavioral Science*, Vol. 5, 1960.

portant for value theory, although not included in his investigation. He further suggests that what he calls "pathic" ways of life may not be basic alternatives to the "healthy" ways, but rather special forms of the latter.

In my opinion, some such limitations are almost inevitable in questionnaire (or related technique) studies of preferences. The range of preferences and the range of cultural, class, biological, and psychological differences affecting them are so great that only certain types of preferences can be handled in any study. That, of course, is nothing to object to unless the inquirer tends to generalize far beyond the range of his findings. Despite the various limitations and problems in Morris' work mentioned so far, I think in many respects his work is useful, and I see no reason to doubt that the type of ratio scale he is interested in can be developed.

However, I am not confident that Morris is as clear as he should be on just what was measured (or in principle could be measured) through the type of technique he used. For example, Morris contrasts, for both semiotic (study of sign behavior) and axiology (study of preferential behavior) the reports of behavior by the behaver himself to a scientific study of that behavior by another observer. He says:

> "In the case of axiology . . . as in the case of semiotic, the scientific approach is in many cases more basic than the approach through self-observation and its reports, since animals and young persons are not able to report their 'values,' and older persons often report them vaguely or even erroneously. One student who said he disliked a certain painting very much was asked why. He said he did not like landscapes. But in the large set of paintings he had been shown, he had given very high preference ratings to a number of landscapes. So even if his statement about disliking the given painting was a correct report of his preferential behavior to it, his reasons given for such behavior were incorrect. It is to be expected that this is the case for much of human preferential behavior."[11]

---

[11]Morris, *Signification and Significance,* p. 17.

I think this shows some confusion, the core of which is that questionnaire, rank-ordering, or paired-comparison techniques will get at some kind of "true" preference that other techniques, such as listening to the behaver's reports on his own behavior, do not get at. Let us assume with Morris that the student mentioned above did give a correct report when he said he disliked a particular landscape painting. How can we conclude that the reason he gave (that he disliked landscapes) is shown to be incorrect because in looking at a large set of paintings he gave high preference ratings to many landscapes? Perhaps *those* ratings were the incorrect ones. Put another way, I am perfectly willing to grant that many people often report their "values" vaguely or even erroneously when asked about them, but why assume that their responses to alternatives in a questionnaire, or to paired comparisons, or to rank-order situations, are more scientific?

In his earlier book, Morris says:

> "Strictly speaking, the respondent in his ratings merely says that he likes each alternative to a certain degree. He may, of course, lie about this, or he may reply as he thinks it is wise to reply in case his identity is known or might become known, or he may put down ratings without even reading the document. All such actions undoubtedly do at times occur. But the size and consistency of, say, the United States sample and the fact that for the most part the replies are voluntary and unsigned make serious worries on this point seem out of place."[12]

But here again we face an old problem — is the respondent indicating a choice he would make if he could freely select from presented alternatives, or is he instead telling us something about his "self-image," or what kinds of choices he would like himself to make, etc.? One need not postulate dishonesty to say that often we cannot ascertain what type of preference is being expressed by a given respondent.

Depending on the purposes of investigation, we might want to know which of several alternatives a person actually would

---

12Morris, *Varieties of Human Value*, p. 13.

choose, or which he says he would choose, or something else. What I object to is not that any of those possibilities is focused on in a particular inquiry, but to the assumption that somehow "truer" preferences are revealed in questionnaire responses than in other types of elicited behavior. Putting the matter more generally, I think it is mistaken to contrast a "scientific" approach to "self-reports" in the way Morris seems inclined to do. In self-reports, questionnaire responses, ratings of paintings, etc., some preference is attributed to the respondent, and the scientific question is the kind of warrant for that attribution of preference.

G. NEEDS

A major tendency among contemporary Anglo-American philosophers is to emphasize the ordinary language uses of various terms and to take such uses as touchstones when criticizing various hypotheses or conclusions about many aspects of human behavior. Since my approach is quite different, some account of it may be helpful before discussing needs and values directly.

In my opinion, the ordinary language uses of many terms often reflect assumptions, theoretical commitments, or conclusions about human behavior that may be mistaken. For example, some ways in which many members of our culture talk about free will are incompatible with reasonably warranted scientific findings about human behavior. More generally, much of our language reflects a sharp mind-body dualism, and a sharp separation between man and his environment, which I regard as not in accord with reasonably sound scientific conclusions. There is nothing surprising in such disparities, since many notions about human behavior that are deeply entrenched in our language were developed long before the rise of scientific inquiry. In recent philosophical discussions, one way of supporting a fundamental distinction between mind and body is to show how much ordinary language would have to be changed if that distinction were eliminated. In my opinion, that is simply putting the cart before the horse; scientific evidence is surely of greater significance than linguistic tradition.

The approach I advocate is to begin with ordinary language uses as data, but then to scrutinize as critically as possible those data and introduce changes in the uses of terms which seem profitable, productive, or warranted as behavioral inquiry proceeds. In talking about 'need,' then, we want that term to refer to much the same field as it does in nontechnical, "folk," or ordinary language, but still to develop its specification in the light of the best results of relevant behavioral inquiries. Just as 'atom' has been given different specifications as physical science has progressed, so 'need' may have its referent changed through time. Another point requiring strong emphasis in view of current philosophical trends is that in no sense am I advocating a final, definitive or unmodifiable specification or clarification of any term. Indeed, my aim in one sense is just the opposite; as our inquiries proceed, we can hope for further improvements. So many philosophers engage in a form of the "quest for certainty" in their discussions of language that it is important to note a very different attitude is adopted here.

Turning now to 'need,' many conflicting uses for that term have been proposed in the behavioral science literature. One tendency is to use 'need' to refer to some kind of lack or imbalance thought to occur strictly "within" the organism, with a sharp separation between organism and environment implied. Another tendency is again to focus on a presumed "inner" state, but to use 'need' to refer to some experience the organism has that is believed to be correlated with the lack. Another approach is to use 'need' as the name for the organism's tendency to persist toward a goal object or situation, or to avoid some other object or situation.[13]

Such considerations involve us in another controversial issue about the use of 'behavior' and the locus of behavior. One approach often found locates behavior strictly within the organism, while the biosocial or transactional approach views behavior as a product of organism and environment. The latter point of view is adopted here.

---

[13]Examples of what can be found in the literature are discussed in Handy, *op. cit.*, pp. 146-152.

Another controversy concerns physiological behavior. Some writers restrict 'need' to physiological imbalances. Others use the term more broadly, but say that physiological needs are prepotent or that in a hierarchical ordering of needs the physiological needs are basic and fundamental. Doubtless different uses of 'prepotent' can be found, but at least frequently the notion encountered is that when there is a conflict of needs, the prepotent one will be satisfied first or most fully.

My view is that what is sound in such approaches is simply that many needs cannot be satisfied at all if physiological needs are not at least minimally satisfied; e.g., a dead man is not going to write books. On the other hand, there are occasions on which humans will starve rather than give up the satisfaction of "acquired" or "secondary" or "tertiary" needs. As Norman Cameron says:

> ". . . we continually meet with situations in which such obviously learned needs as those for social or economic security, for approval and acceptance, for human company, for prestige and for esteem actually crowd out hunger, thirst and sex-need. Indeed, the individual variations in need prepotency from person to person, and in the same person from time to time, tend to make the question of need-satisfaction supremacy an individual and a temporal matter, rather than a fixed and universal principle."[14]

I propose using 'need' to refer to an unstable or disturbed equilibrium in behavior, with behavior taken not as something within the organism strictly, but as part of the organic-environmental situation. The location of needs strictly within the organism seems to me to generate problems, because right from birth we have needs that can be satisfied only by the environment, such as those for oxygen, fluids, food, protection against excessive heat and cold, etc. Moreover, for humans the satisfaction of needs frequently is impossible without the aid of other persons. If we look at behavioral transactions as they occur, then, we see that needs require the environment for their satisfaction and directly or indirectly require the help of other humans. In

---

[14]Norman Cameron, *The Psychology of Behavior Disorders*, Boston, Houghton Mifflin, 1947, p. 126.

my opinion, the need satisfaction process literally is biosocial. A methodological approach that begins with the assumption of a fundamental separation between the individual and the group, and between the individual and his environment, then has to develop an "apparatus" for bringing the assumed separates together. Why not begin the inquiry with what we observe: biosocial or transactional processes?

On the view adopted here, need generation is characteristic of all ongoing behavior, including symbolic or sign behavior. As humans develop and become involved in new transactions, new needs are developed and so-called prepotencies change. Rather than an atomistic approach in which some hierarchical pattern of needs is postulated, a holistic and dynamic approach is taken.

Finally, I put strong emphasis on needs as producing further behavior. When the behavioral equilibrium becomes unstable, the organism shows marked activity aimed at restoring the equilibrium, including selective or preferential responses.

The way I propose to use 'need' is summed up in the following quotation:

> " 'Need' is the label adopted here for an unstable or disturbed equilibrium in behavior. . . . [B]ehavior is taken *not* as of the organism alone but as of the organic-environmental situation. These organic-environmental instabilities, which are found throughout adjustive behavior (including sign-behavior), typically are accompanied by increased or protracted activity and tension. The behavior concerned may focus on the achievement of some goal object or on the avoidance of some object or situation. Preferences are displayed, the responses made are selective, and the outcome is a restoration of equilibrium or its stabilization (e.g., release of tension, quiescence)."[15]

To reemphasize and restate a point made earlier, this proposed use of 'need' is *not* offered either as an analysis of the ordinary language use of that term or as an account of how behavioral scientists typically use it. (For other views of needs, see Chapter III, Section D and Chapter V, Section B.) Rather, it is proposed as a useful hypothesis on the basis of what can be

---

[15]Handy, *op. cit.*, p. 151.

observed about certain pervasive aspects of human behavior. In any event, the processes involved are the important thing, not the particular label chosen. Perhaps some term other than 'need' might be more appropriate for those processes, or perhaps those processes are poorly or mistakenly described here. What I say, then, is intended as an hypothesis, not as any final, or near final, solution or clarification.

H. NEEDS AND VALUES

A major theme of this book is that since 'value' is used in a great many different and conflicting ways, if the term is to be retained we should give it a specification that is in accord with whatever warranted assertions are available about the behavior involved.

One problem I wish to avoid is an unwarranted hypostatization or reification of value phenomena. In some theories that put major emphasis on 'value' as a noun, hypostatization may occur. Here the major emphasis is on the valuing transaction. This, of course, is taken as a behavioral process, not as something that is unamenable to scientific inquiry. Within that setting, 'value' is taken as an object (in a broad sense of 'object'), but this is *not* to confer either some special ontological status on values nor to deemphasize in any way the behavioral transactions involved.

Some writers have maintained that focusing on 'value' rather than on 'valuing' not only may involve reification, but an illegitimate assumption that values can be observed and measured. For example, Kenneth Boulding, after commenting that such phrases as '*it* is raining' refer to processes that do not involve an *it* at all, says:

> "The word 'values' is almost as bad as 'it.' Grammatically it is a noun and hence we expect it to be a thing. The search for a thing called a value, however, is likely to be fruitless, for the context refers not to a thing which can be observed, weighed and measured, but to a process, the process of valuation."[16]

---

[16]Kenneth E. Boulding, "Divine Legitimation and the Defense Establishment," *The Humanist*, Vol. XXVIII, 1968, p. 21.

On the view proposed here, a value can be observed and measured, as one aspect of the transactional process.

As will be recalled, for R. B. Perry 'X is valuable' = 'interest is taken in X.' In a similar context, the view proposed here is that 'X is a generic value' = 'X satisfies a need.' 'Satisfies' here is to be interpreted broadly and generally. Both actual and potential satisfactions are included; temporary satiation for X does not result in X's ceasing to be valuable (e.g., food is a value even for those who are not hungry at the moment). Something that could satisfy a need, but which is not so recognized, would be a value (as in nutritional deficiencies of which the person is unaware). And a contemplated but unperformed deed could be called valuable if it would satisfy a need when performed.

If this proposal is accepted, statements about values are in principle descriptive and testable. Value statements are "objective" in the sense that whether or not X is a value is not dependent on the "subjective" opinions, feelings, attitudes, etc., of an individual or a group. On the other hand, values are not absolute in the sense some have argued; there can be variation in needs among individuals, in different historical periods, and in different cultural settings. Although presumably some needs may be the same in all cultures and for all humans historically, other needs may differ markedly.

Moreover, not only can needs conflict, both for individuals and for groups, but many alternative ways of satisfying a given need may be possible and conflicts can also arise among those alternatives. In a complete value theory, ways of handling such conflicts, the establishment of priorities, etc., would be called for. At the present, such topics will not be discussed; the focus here is only on what Perry called "generic" value.

Despite my view that ordinary language is not the touchstone for arriving at the specification of a term, and despite the fact that many writers on value theory have used 'value' in different and inconsistent ways, I believe the use of 'value' proposed here refers to much the same field as that term does both in ordinary language and in many value theories.

For example, often in discussions about values a central

theme is the "push" we feel in the direction of certain objects and the aversion we feel toward others. The "imperativeness" often associated with values has sometimes been attributed to a nonbehavioral source, especially in theories that oppose the adequacy of scientific inquiry into values. On the view proposed here, that "push" or imperativeness is taken as directly rooted in fundamental adjustive behavior. If we take account of evolutionary processes, we can understand why certain needs are so strong, so urgent, and so imperious. For excellent biosocial reasons, humans are strongly for some things and strongly against others. Either individuals or groups can "go wrong" in the sense of favoring something that leads either to unnecessary need frustration or in opposing what would lead to need satisfaction. Such "wrong" behavior, however, is also amenable to description and prediction through scientific inquiry.

In general, the selective-rejective behavior characteristic of need satisfaction sequences is just what many behavioral scientists apparently have focused on in their studies of values, since that behavior exhibits preferences, selective responses, etc. The organism may or may not be fully aware (or aware at all) of his preferences or what his needs are, so in the theory proposed here there is no restriction of 'value' to what a person "consciously" or "deliberately" selects or prefers or desires. At the same time, at least in principle the need theory allows for differentiating between what will satisfy a need and what will not (and for different degrees of the adequacy of need satisfaction), and thus for "objectivity" and "rationality."

In relation to ordinary language, it seems to me that most of the things that we might call valuable are also things that satisfy needs (as 'need' is used here). This is not, of course, to say that people *mean* 'X satisfies a need' when they say 'X is valuable,' but rather that the fields of reference are similar. Even if that is not so, however, the need theory might have other virtues that would make further exploration profitable. In any event, the aim here has been to focus on a certain type of behavioral transaction that often is taken as a value context both in "folk" language and in behavioral science inquiries, and then to look for suitable specifications of key terms in the description of those transactions.

I. MEASUREMENT OF NEED SATISFACTION TRANSACTIONS

In my opinion, if needs are taken as construed here all the significant aspects of a value transaction can be measured in principle. Let us focus first on the disturbance in equilibrium. For physiological needs such as hunger or thirst, with presently available techniques many significant measurements of such disturbances seem possible. As we shift to types of behavior other than the physiological, existing techniques of measurement may be far less adequate, and quite possibly for some types of behavior we at present have no useful mensurational techniques.

If we focus next on 'value' as the object satisfying a need, often we already have quite adequate measurements. Assuming we have been able to assess accurately some nutritional deficiency, we can measure the extent to which the deficiency is remedied by some particular nutrient. In some nonphysiological areas, we also already have fairly useful measures of how adequately some object may satisfy a particular need, although in other areas we may have nothing that facilitates measurement even in the broadest sense.

If we focus on the selective-rejective aspects of a valuing transaction, and the exhibiting of preferences, here again we find a wide range of possibilities. There seems little doubt that a human's food preferences, for example, can be measured quite accurately in a controlled experiment. And in cases where a direct measure of actual food choices is not possible, we have noted a variety of questionnaire and other techniques through which verbal responses about preferences can be measured. We have also discussed some problems with the measurements of preferences, and there may well be some preferences that are extremely difficult to measure in any sense.

If we focus on the quiescence aspects of a valuing transaction, again there are instances in which we can measure quite precisely what is involved, as in the changes some drug will produce in reducing muscle cramps or the like. The resolution of an acutely felt conflict of loyalties might be far more difficult to measure, but again, so long as the emphasis is on behavior, nothing that is totally impossible to measure in principle seems to be involved.

The general point is that on the need theory, in contrast to some other value theories, there is no one neat sense in which value phenomena are measurable. Which aspect or aspects of a value transaction are of concern may vary from inquiry to inquiry. Instead of a single metric through which all values can be measured, on the proposed theory a variety of metrics would be needed, depending on what aspects of the transaction are of interest in a particular inquiry. Given present technological facilities, it seems to me that we have a wide range of situations, from those in which some aspects of a transaction are as precisely measurable as many phenomena in the natural sciences to those in which there are no techniques that are even roughly suitable for what we want to measure. Rather than developing a single technique, or a small group of techniques, fundamental for the measurement of value, the problem is to find appropriate ways of measuring different aspects of value transactions.

In addition, I suggest that at least some of the confusion and incoherence often found in discussions of value measurement would be lessened if the proposed theory were adopted, since in any one instance we would then be focusing on a particular type of restoration of a particular unstable behavioral equilibrium; i.e., on the satisfaction of a need.

Since I have taken value to be "objective" in the sense that whatever does satisfy a need is a generic value, we are not faced immediately (as some theories are) with the question of how to measure "subjective" entities, although some of the ways of measuring those entities may prove useful in measuring certain aspects of value transactions. Nor are we restricted to verbal behavior, as some investigators are, although again some measurements of verbal responses may be highly useful.

Summing up, the only limitation on the measurement of any aspect of a value transaction, according to my theory, would be any limitation that might exist on the measurement of behavior. If behavior is construed as it is here, I see no such limitation in principle. The frequent emphasis I have placed on "in principle" in no sense is intended to slide over, ignore, or minimize technical or practical difficulties; frequently there is scant consolation in the fact that something can be measured in principle if in practice we can't measure it at all. On the other hand, since traditionally so many have urged some "in principle" limitation, it may be worthwhile to be freed from such views. Indeed, I might record here my belief that the great difficulty in so many alleged measurements of value is not that any difficulties in principle are involved, or that some modification in basic scientific methodology is required, but simply that the alleged measurements are so poor and unimpressive in practice.

J. COMPARISON OF PREFERENCES AND NEEDS

In both Morris' theory and mine the field of concern is selective-rejective behavior, but we disagree about which aspect or aspects of that field to label 'value.' One basic choice to be made is whether it is best to use 'value' as a label for anything that is selected or rejected (allowing 'value' to include 'disvalues'), or whether only some things that are or could be selected or rejected are to be given that label. (This is the cluster of issues discussed often under the headings of the preferred vs. the preferable, the desired vs. the desirable, the objectively valuable vs. the subjectively valuable, etc.)

Morris, it will be recalled, distinguished between operative values (what is preferred), conceived values (what is regarded as preferable), and object values (what is actually preferable). Since on his view all three types of values are to be explicated with respect to some form of the term 'prefer,' Morris is in agreement with those who hold that any preference is a value, but he also allows for a strong contrast between the preferred and the preferable. It should be noted that Morris does not regard his three types of values as ontologically distinct; the different uses of 'value' refer not to "different entities," but rather to "different aspects of the value field."[17]

I see two difficulties in Morris' approach, one related to problems in the empirical differentiation between the three types of value, and one in his theoretical structure.

As will be recalled, Morris saw the Ways to Live instrument as primarily measuring conceived values, and in comparing results obtained on that instrument with results obtained through the Allport-Vernon-Lindzey test, suggested that the latter basically measured operative values. But the distinction between operative and conceived values seems difficult to pin down if questionnaires are used as the measuring instrument. Clearly, both the Ways to Live document and the Allport-Vernon-Lindzey test measure what individuals say their preferences are. This might indicate that both are dealing with conceived values, although as Morris notes, his instrument has the values more "conceptualized" than does the other test. And in both tests some subjects may respond, not in terms of either what they actually would choose or what they believe is preferable, but in terms of what they regard as politic to select.

Further, Morris says very little about the criteria for determining what actually is preferable (object values), and it is difficult for me to see how he can get at such values through his questionnaire. This is not to say that Morris' tripartite classification of 'value' could not be useful; the point at the moment is that his way of measuring values does not, in my opinion, lend itself to the kind of distinction he makes in his classification.

The second difficulty relates to his insistence that all three types of value are best explicated with respect to some form of the term 'prefer.' Some writers maintain that much of the trouble in value theory stems from the fact that 'preferred' and 'preferable' are verbally so similar, but that the referents of those terms are so different. Far from it being a virtue to link together all three of Morris' values through some form of 'prefer,' they would regard that as a basic source of difficulty. Such critics are inclined to restrict value to what is preferable.

---

[17]Morris, *Varieties of Human Value*, p. 12.

In the need theory proposed here, the decision was made to identify 'value' with 'what satisfies a need,' even if the person or group involved does not prefer, or does not even know of the existence of, what would satisfy the need. However, emphasis is placed on the generation of preferences in valuing transactions; the preferences exhibited were not taken as values, but as typical aspects of adjustive behavior. Such an approach would avoid some of the problems Morris has, although obviously the need theory is not in accord with uses of 'value' that identify values and preferences.

Morris himself has stated some of the main differences between preferences and needs. He agrees with Dewey and others that selective-rejective behavior helps maintain an organism's life processes, and then says:

> "This fact requires a distinction between preferential behavior and need-reducing behavior. For, while in general an organism's selections and rejections do tend to be controlled by and to minister to its motivating drives, preferred objects may not in fact satisfy those drives, or at least not satisfy them as fully as would other objects. Organisms do tend to select those objects, and those modes of action upon objects, which satisfy their motivations more fully than do other objects and modes of action. . . . But this process of correcting preferences requires experimentation, flexibility, and time. Even in very adaptable organisms preferred objects or actions seldom satisfy existing needs completely, and in the case of the culturally deviant person or the psychotic, the gap may be very great. A society may through its educative process perpetuate preferential behavior when such behavior is not adequate to the needs of its members. And the evaluation of an object by an organism may be wrong in the sense that the signified preferential status of an object or act may not accord with its actual ability to satisfy a given need. Hence an organism may, because of its evaluation of something, accord to an object or act a preferential status which is harmful to the attainment of its ends."[18]

---

[18]Charles Morris, "Axiology as the Science of Preferential Behavior," in Ray Lepley, ed., *Value: A Cooperative Inquiry*, New York, Columbia University Press, 1949, pp. 215-216.

I think Morris is basically correct in indicating some of the main differences between needs and preferences. Obviously, such differences in and of themselves do not show it is more productive to focus on needs as basic to values than on preferences. But in handling conflicts of values, in establishing priorities, in developing social policy, etc., I suggest that it is advantageous to take needs as central to values, since they are more fundamental in behavior, more stable, and more important to the organism. In addition, predicting the relevant human behavior and finding ways of changing behavior that is inappropriate or inadequate is, I think, facilitated by emphasizing needs, in that both "good" and "bad" patterns of behavior seem more easily describable and controllable than if preferences are taken as central. For example, a heroin addict's satisfying of his needs through narcotics is best viewed as an inadequate, self-defeating, and dangerous behavioral pattern. A grasp of the "if. . . then" sequences under which such behavior occurs and how it can be changed seems more productive than viewing that behavior as a preference for what is not preferable.

However, the stability and priority of needs over preferences mentioned above could be exaggerated, for on the view of needs adopted here some needs are close to what others call preferences. If one used 'need' so that there were a very few needs arranged in a hierarchical order, and if that approach corresponded to what could be observed in the relevant behavior, then empirically there might be a sharp distinction between needs and preferences. However, when one takes needs to be as encompassing and as flexible as is done here, need satisfaction sequences cover what some other writers refer to as preferences. In any event, the unsettled terminology (unsettled when we take account of what behavior is being referred to) plagues this whole area of inquiry.

Some writers would oppose the broad use of 'need' proposed here, and even see harmful social consequences flowing from that broad use. David Braybrooke, for example, has argued that the "overextension of the concept of need" may "inhibit the exercise of freedom in the development of preferences." He distinguishes between "course-of-life" needs, "which people have all through

their lives or at certain stages of life through which all must pass"
(e.g., shelter, clothing, rest, etc.) and "adventitious" needs, "which
come and go with particular contingent projects" (e.g., a burglar's
need for a jimmy, a student's need for a letter of recommenda-
tion).[19]

On the use of 'need' I proposed, Braybrooke's adventitious
needs would often be as important as his course-of-life needs; as
argued, a learned need may be as important as, or more important
than, food for a particular individual. Braybrooke emphasizes
several times that needs have priority over preferences, and therefore that the extension of needs reduces the role of preferences.
If something is (in his framework) more properly regarded as a
preference than as a need, it would not necessarily take priority
over other preferences.

Without going into this issue in detail, since my main reason
for raising it is to illustrate some of the complex terminological
and methodological problems, it seems to me that both for individuals and for groups a pressing problem often is to decide which
unstable equilibrium is to be restored, or to what degree it is to be
restored. In that process some of what I call preferences may be
mistaken, in the ways Morris mentions, and therefore can be dis-
counted or ignored. (We may, of course, also be mistaken about
needs.)

Both Braybrooke and I agree that needs should take priority
over preferences; we disagree on the range of needs and which
label to apply to which forms of behavior. Partly, of course, the
issue is terminological, but also there are differences as to what
behavior is empirically. In general, terminological, methodological, and evidential questions flow together in this area of inquiry
and are mutually related. In any event, I see the main issue not
as which label is most appropriate, but as how best to describe
and predict the behavior involved.

In summary, the hypothesis offered here is that emphasizing
needs rather than preferences may produce greater clarity in value

---

[19]David Braybrooke, "Let Needs Diminish that Preferences May Prosper," in
Nicholas Rescher, ed., *Studies in Moral Philosophy (American Philosophical Quarterly* Monograph Series, No. 1) Oxford, Basil Blackwell, 1968, pp. 90-91, p. 100.

theory, may make it easier to develop scientifically warranted assertions about the behavior involved, and may help focus more effectively on which aspects of valuing transactions we are measuring in a given inquiry.

Chapter IX

CONCLUSION

A. OVERVIEW

We have considered various issues in measurement theory, especially alleged differences in the measurement of physical and behavioral phenomena; some analyses of 'value' in terms of interests, preferences, needs, and selective systems; several attempts to measure values; and methodological controversies associated with all the issues just mentioned.

Measurement is viewed here as a form of behavior designed to help ascertain reliably and accurately the "if. . . then" relations characteristic of the processes into which we are inquiring, including behavioral processes. From that point of view, in this final chapter some general criticisms of attempts to measure values will be considered and some of the book's main theses will be reviewed. For convenience, the critics will be divided into two categories, with no implication that the categories are exhaustive or mutually exclusive. Some critics maintain that values in principle cannot be measured, while others maintain that alleged measurements of value are trivial, misguided, invalid, or otherwise defective.

B. VALUES IN PRINCIPLE CANNOT BE MEASURED

Historically in our civilization, one group of writers has maintained that at least certain values cannot be scientifically measured because they are not natural entities having a spatio-temporal locus. Sometimes values are said to be mystically apprehended, and sometimes to be knowable through a special intellectual faculty, but in either case values are thought to transcend the world of objects that can be measured scientifically. Such views raise interesting questions about human knowing, about the composition of the cosmos, and about appropriate investigative methods, but in this book little direct attention was given to arguments that values are transcendent. However, it was noted that some people, when asked, are quite willing to rank comparatively even what they regard as "infinite" values, which implies at least a crude form of measurement.

The approach adopted here was to emphasize the importance and usefulness of first indicating what the value field is behaviorally, and then to inquire into what aspects of that field can be measured, and through what techniques. Even if many aspects of that behavior can be usefully measured, other "transcendent values" may of course exist that cannot be so measured. Since our focus is on value processes that are located in the natural world, those general issues will not be discussed further.

Another tradition is found among those who do not insist on a special ontological status for values, and who may indeed be perfectly willing to say that valuing is a natural, this-worldly process. But they construe values as "subjective" entities that cannot be measured satisfactorily compared to the "fundamental" measurement possible in physical inquiry.

It was argued here that the fundamentalist approach encounters the same type of "subjectivity" when the entire measuring transaction is considered. The formal characteristics of the dimensions involved, or the scales developed, may meet certain logical requirements fully, but to ascertain whether or not actual measurements or measuring processes conform to those logical requirements involves behavior that according to some fundamentalists is subjective. If we take as our criterion measurement in practice, the formal beauty and virtue of "fundamental" techniques, scales, etc., may have little significance.

When measurement is viewed in the context of developing

more accurate and precise ways to describe, predict, and control aspects and phases of the cosmos, the test of particular modes and methods of measurement is "pragmatic." Logically or formally impressive techniques that cannot be applied fruitfully are, from that perspective, inferior to other techniques that do have a fruitful application. Moreover, what is fruitful depends on the level of development achieved. At one historical stage, measurements that are crude, imperfect, and deficient as compared to what will be achieved in a later stage of development may still mark a considerable advance in man's ability to describe and predict. To insist *a priori* that all mensurational techniques be judged primarily in terms of their logical structure seems irrelevant and often foolish.

Of course, one could insist on restricting the term 'measurement' to particular processes that have been successful in physical inquiry, and then use some other label for certain kinds of quantification of aspects of human behavior. Some version of that approach has been taken not only by many behavioral scientists, but by philosophers of quite different persuasions. R. B. Perry, for example, does not insist that values are quantitatively measurable in the same way that physical science phenomena are, and says that it is optional whether we broaden the sense of 'measurement' used in physical inquiry or develop some new terminology. And Bergmann and Spence argue that it is preferable to use 'quantification' rather than 'measurement' in psychophysical contexts. On their view, quantification in psychophysics cannot "without violence" be subsumed "under any of the customary classifications of physical measurement." They go on to say that no "disparagement of the psychophysical scales is involved in their being set aside from physical measurement."[1]

To discuss such issues intelligently, we need to consider both the most appropriate use of 'measurement' and methodological and empirical questions about what behavior is being measured

---

[1] R. B. Perry, *Realms of Value*, Cambridge, Harvard University Press, 1954, p. 52. Gustav Bergmann and Kenneth W. Spence, "The Logic of Psychophysical Measurement," *Psychological Review*, Vol. 51, 1944; reprinted as "Psychophysical Measurement" in Melvin H. Marx, ed., *Psychological Theory*, New York, Macmillan, 1951. The references are to p. 267 and p. 275 of Marx.

or quantified. The view adopted here is that if measurement is taken in its full transactional context as a way of providing important warranted information, both the logical structure or ordering of that information, and the operations through which it is gained and transmitted, are important. The effectiveness of measurement is to be judged in terms of all the relevant scientific information we possess and thus involves the funded scientific findings available at any given time.

Moreover, as argued in Chapter II, in carrying out measurements in physical inquiry psychological and other behavioral considerations are involved in problems of aligning markers, etc. So rather than searching for a once-and-for-all hierarchical ordering of types of measurement (or quantification), a more holistic and contextual approach was suggested. On the basis of that approach, it seemed appropriate to view both physical and behavioral quantifications as types of measurement, without ignoring important differences between them. The test proposed for both areas is the degree to which the measurements are warranted, rather than the specific types of scales or operations used.

From that point of view, various attempts to measure values were described and criticized. The inquiries discussed (as well as other typical inquiries not discussed) dealt with selective-rejective behavior. Views emphasizing the key constituent in that behavior as preferences, interests, needs, and selective systems were discussed. On the theory proposed here, important aspects of all those constituents are measurable. The problem encountered in many inquiries is confusion as to just which aspect or aspects the inquirers measured or thought they had measured. Hence the reiterated theme in this book that terminological clarification is called for in order to assess what has been done, or what could be done, with existing techniques.

The issue becomes especially acute in the work of many behavioral scientists who focus on *preferences* while ignoring differences among types of preference. Often critics complain that the typical techniques for ascertaining preferences used by psychologists or sociologists give no assurance that the preferences exhibited on the test instrument are the same as the preferences the subject would exhibit if he could freely choose among alternatives "in real life." This can be an oversimplified way of approaching the question, for we may want to inquire into many different types of preferences. For example (as noted in Chapter IV, Section H), George Lundberg pointed out that the verbal professions of influential people may have more social significance than the way those people behave in private. For some purposes, then, verbal professions may be exactly what we want to study and measure.

Much controversy ensues over the best way to use some of the terminology in this area and about the type of behavior we are trying to "pin down." For example, Thurstone says:

> "It seems to be rather generally assumed that the validity of an attitude scale, with its verbal statements, must be determined by its agreement with overt conduct. This is a mistaken notion. A man may find it expedient to act in a manner which is not indicative of how he feels. In other situations he may find it expedient to make statements which are inconsistent with his preferences. If there is inconsistency between what a man says about x and what he does about x, which shall we take as indicative of his attitude? Perhaps neither. In such a case I should prefer to find out what he says to his best friends when he is not in danger of being quoted. To me, attitude means primarily how a man feels about any designated psychological object. In practical life he may find it expedient to deviate from his own attitude in his public statements or in his actions. What he says and what he does may both be inconsistent with his feeling about x."[2]

Often the contrast between "overt" behavior and behavior in a questionnaire situation can be quite misleading, and not only because one form of behavior is as overt as the other. All the various forms of behavior may be worth studying. For example, assume that a given individual responds to a questionnaire in terms of the "self-image" he has and that such responses diverge considerably from the behavior he shows in other settings. For

---

[2]L. L. Thurstone, *The Measurement of Values,* Chicago, University of Chicago Press, 1959, p. 321.

some inquiries, it might be precisely such "self-images" that are of interest, and quite possibly reliable information about them will help predict *some* types of behavior. So in that instance disparity between verbalized statements of preference and some other evincing of preference will not matter. Sometimes, indeed, what is marked on a paper may be exactly what is most important; in an election, who is elected depends on what choices are made on the ballot, not the "inner feelings" of the voters. However, in other situations, such deviance would be highly important; for example, if questionnaire studies of consumer preferences are intended to help predict what will be bought, marked disparity between buying behavior and what is indicated on the questionnaire is important.

To sum up, the view adopted here (and for which support has been given throughout the book) is that all of the aspects of behavior various inquirers have taken as constitutive of value are measurable in principle; the difficulty is that so often it is far from clear just which aspect has been measured. The results obtained may be useful and important for description and prediction even if those results do not meet certain tests that are commonly met in some types of physical measurement.

As an illustration, sometimes a great to-do is made about the fact that in behavioral measurements equality of score differences cannot be interpreted in the way that equality of differences are interpreted in physical contexts. As Bergmann and Spence point out, however, such behavioral measurements may be important:

> "Assume that a property is, in a statistically stable manner, distributed over a large population and that a percentile scale has been based, in the familiar fashion, upon the area under that curve. The question then arises as to what meaning can be attributed to the numerical equality of score differences, such as, let us say, between 60 and 50, and 25 and 15 respectively. Despite the opinion current among psychologists that this numerical equality does not signify 'equality,' it does have a well defined empirical meaning, namely this: in any fair sample the number of individuals between 60 and 50 is equal to the number of individuals between 25 and 15."[3]

---

[3]Bergmann and Spence, *op. cit.*, p. 266.

I would only add that if we want to find out about the number of individuals in those categories, then the scaling was successful and we might as well call it measurement.

In short, the success of value measurement depends on how well it aids us in describing and predicting human behavior that is taken as value behavior. Those who refuse to call "value" anything that can be measured are welcome to their terminological decisions, but that does not keep selective-rejective behavior from being measurable.

C.   VALUE MEASUREMENTS ARE TRIVIAL

A second major type of criticism is that the values which are measured by behavioral scientists are trivial and that existing mensurational techniques are inappropriate for more significant values. For example, such a critic might say that it is no surprise to find that menu choices in a cafeteria setting can be measured, but that this really doesn't tell us very much about important human values; behavioral scientists involved in menu-type measurements are either wasting their time or are confusing such preferences with more significant values.

One reply that has been made is to point out that techniques and methods can be tested and further developed in investigations of relatively trivial matters, and I think there is considerable merit in that contention. (But we obviously cannot just assume that what is successful in trivial areas of concern will necessarily be useful in more important areas.) Also, accusations of triviality sometimes may be merely a cover for an unwarranted but rigidly held conviction that no vital human values are measurable.

On the other hand, and without condemning many of the value measurements that have been made, I think there often is an unwarranted and self-defeating inflation of the significance of what has been achieved. Rather simple and uncritically done work on occasion is discussed pretentiously, as though a great breakthrough had resulted. So, without agreeing at all with the underlying themes of many critics who maintain that scientific measures of value are trivial, I do take a rather skeptical attitude toward what has been achieved to date.

To illustrate, some work of Milton Rokeach will be discussed. He indicates deep dissatisfaction with conventional social psychology. The "great majority of experimental findings" on attitude change, he says, actually have little to do with attitude change, and a simpler way can be found to account for the results. Rokeach believes the "time is now perhaps ripe" to shift the main focus in social psychology away from attitude organization and to study instead value organization and change. This presupposes a "clear-cut conceptual distinction between attitude and value," although he emphasizes also that beliefs, attitudes, and values "form a functionally integrated cognitive system."[4]

Rokeach differentiates between 'value' and 'attitude' as follows:

"An attitude . . . is an organization of several beliefs focused on a specific object (physical or social, concrete or abstract) or situation, predisposing one to respond in some preferential manner. Some of these beliefs about an object or situation concern matters of fact and others concern matters of evaluation. . . . Values, on the other hand, have to do with modes of conduct and end-states of existence. To say that a person 'has a value' is to say that he has an enduring belief that a specific mode of conduct or end-state of existence is personally and socially preferable to alternative modes of conduct or end-states of existence. . . . While an attitude represents several beliefs focused on a single specific object or situation, a value is a single belief that transcendentally guides action and judgments across specific objects and situations, and beyond immediate goals to more ultimate end-states of existence. Moreover, a value, unlike an attitude, is an imperative to action, not only a belief about the preferable but also a preference for the preferable."[5]

He further distinguishes between "instrumental" and "terminal" values. In his formulation, an instrumental value is a "single

[4]Milton Rokeach, *Beliefs, Attitudes, and Values,* San Francisco, Jossey-Bass, 1968, pp. ix-xii.
[5]*Ibid.,* pp. 159-160.

belief" that a specific mode of conduct (the value) is "personally and socially preferable in all situations with respect to all objects," and a terminal value is a belief that "an end-state of existence" (the value) is "personally and socially worth striving for." (His formulation of the distinction is different from those often found.)

He then describes his current research program. His first problem was to find a way to measure value systems, and he describes his approach as "extremely simple." Initially, he took a dozen of what he called instrumental values (e.g., *broadminded, forgiving, responsible*) and a dozen terminal values (e.g., *equality, freedom, salvation*), alphabetized each set, and asked his subjects to rank-order them in importance. After improving the items, he got data on the instrumental and terminal value rank-orderings of many groups differing in age, sex, education, etc.

In his discussion of the validity of his instrument, Rokeach makes much of the finding that the ranking of one terminal value alone, *salvation,* "highly predicts church attendance." Those who reported they were sympathetic to and participated in civil rights demonstrations tended to rank *freedom* first, and *equality* third, among 12 terminal values. Unemployed Negroes ranked *freedom* tenth and *equality* first. Students at a Calvinist college ranked both *freedom* and *equality* relatively low. Many similar results were obtained, and Rokeach is optimistic about the validity of his research.

He further says that his data on *freedom* and *equality* point to "the presence of a simple, nonetheless comprehensive, two-dimensional model for describing all the major variations among various political orientations." To illustrate the model, he compares it to the four points of a compass. The north pole represents those who value highly both *freedom* and *equality* (he lists here liberal democrats, socialists, and humanists); the south pole represents those putting a low value on both (he lists fascists, Nazis, and Ku Klux Klan members); the east is the location of those who value *freedom* highly and put a low value on *equality* (John Birch Society, conservative Republicans, followers of Ayn Rand); and on the west are those who put a high value on *equality* and a low value on *freedom* (Stalinists and Maoists).

In support of this model, Rokeach cites a word-count technique: 25,000-word samples were selected from political writings representing the four poles, and a count was made of the number of times various terminal and instrumental values were favorably mentioned. (Samples came from socialist writers such as Norman Thomas and Erich Fromm, from Hitler, Barry Goldwater, and Lenin.) The socialists mentioned *freedom* favorably 66 times and *equality* 62 times, and ranked *freedom* first and *equality* second in a group of 17 terminal values. In Hitler's *Mein Kampf*, *freedom* was ranked 16th and *equality* 17th among the same 17 terminal values. For Goldwater, *freedom* was first and *equality* 16th; for Lenin, *freedom* was 17th and *equality* first. Rokeach says: "All in all, these data seem to fit the two-dimensional model almost perfectly."

At the end of the chapter Rokeach says:

> "As I conclude this chapter I become acutely aware of at least a few questions that should be raised about the methods and findings reported here. Do the various value terms have the same meaning for different subjects? What ethical precautions are especially necessary in research on value change? Are the systematic value and attitude changes and the sleeper effects reported here genuine changes or are they artifacts of the experimental situation? Can we expect behavioral changes to follow from such value and attitude changes? Is it just as consistent for a person to move *freedom* down to *equality* as to move *equality* up to *freedom*? . . . What are the implications of our formulations and findings for education, therapy, and other areas of human concern that necessarily engage people's values?"[6]

Since the research discussed here is not presented fully by Rokeach (he promises a fuller report in a subsequent publication), it may not be fair to criticize him on the basis of the materials presently available. Yet the hubris exhibited is rather remarkable, and helps to illustrate why some critics are unimpressed by alleged measurements of value. Starting with a very simple and in many ways questionable instrument, we are quickly plunged into broad questions about implications for education, therapy, etc.

[6]*Ibid.*, p. 178.

The apparent lack of self-criticism in some parts of his work is also notable. Translation problems alone might suggest some caution in comparing word counts of the terms 'freedom' and 'equality' in the writings of Hitler and Lenin to those of American authors, let alone the notorious problems about the referents of those terms in English. Indeed, the various semantic and terminological problems are acute throughout Rokeach's research. Further, one would like evidence for the notion that a value, taken as an "enduring belief" that something is "personally and socially preferable" to its alternatives, can be gotten at through word counts, rank-ordering of a selected group of words, or similar procedures.

Many writers maintain that there can be a great difference between what is taken as personally preferable and what is socially preferable, but Rokeach insists (by definition) that a value is not a value unless both are involved. Interesting questions occur also about the sense in which values such as *freedom* and *equality* are single beliefs rather than composites of beliefs, especially since that distinction is basic for Rokeach's differentiation between 'attitude' and 'value,' which in turn is important for his proposed reform of social psychology.

Without dwelling further on possible criticisms, and without denying some merits in Rokeach's research program, his project appears to be an attempt to arrive at highly significant results about complex human behavior through a very simple approach that either bypasses many pertinent issues or glosses over them. The great danger in such approaches, in my opinion, is not that the unwary will be taken in and believe there is a strong scientific warrant for the results, but rather that those negatively disposed toward a scientific inquiry into values will interpret such attempts as a kind of *reductio ad absurdum* of any scientific approach. Such considerations raise the general question of the "validity" of various measurements of value, a topic to which we will now turn.

D. VALIDITY OF VALUE MEASUREMENTS

As argued so often in this book, a marked feature of much discussion about the measurement of values is vagueness, incoherence, and confusion as to how 'value' is being used in a given inquiry. The official definitions given sometimes do not conform to what was studied, and there often appears to be little effective control over what putatively was measured.

I suggested that many empirical inquirers have in general focused on the field of selective-rejective behavior, and then concentrated on some subarea of that field for investigation, but without being particularly clear as to just what that subarea was. And yet it seems likely that at least implicitly various investigators had some particular subarea in mind, since often they justify the specific techniques used on the grounds that those techniques are more appropriate than some others.

Before going further, let us review some of the techniques and approaches described earlier. The "values" inquired into ranged from simple tastes to conceptions of the good life. Paired comparisons, rank-orderings, agreement or disagreement with set items, and content analyses of responses to presented materials all were used. Often the test instrument allowed the respondents to indicate their degree of liking and disliking, with different instruments providing a different number of "intensities" to choose among. Some workers believed that questionnaires are not flexible enough for investigating values, and we noted two varieties of the Koloman technique, in one of which the respondents indicated the degree of their agreement or disagreement with a presented passage, and in the other of which content analyses were made of what the respondents said after hearing the presented passage. Another study emphasized clinical interviews and projective test results as well as questionnaire responses.

All these approaches elicit selective-rejective behavior, but presumably rather different forms of such behavior. This makes it extremely difficult to assess comparatively the results of the different types of inquiry. So far as I am aware, there have been few attempts to compare the use of different techniques on the same subjects, although Morris did give the Allport-Vernon-Lindzey test to some of his subjects. I suspect that if more such comparative assessments were made, the results would be rather inconclusive and confusing.

The same point comes out in a different way when one studies the attempts made to validate the particular instruments used. We have seen that sometimes word counts of published materials were used to check on a given technique for measuring values, sometimes clinical procedures, sometimes descriptive literature about the attitudes of the type of subject studied, and sometimes "common sense" notions of what, say, women are like compared to men, or engineers to nonengineers.

Much of the work on value measurement seems to fall into two categories. The first, illustrated by questionnaire type techniques, often runs into the type of problem just mentioned. The second approach, illustrated by Clark Hull's work, is far clearer about what is taken as a value and how theoretically values can be measured, but our present capability for actually measuring values as so construed is very low. To some extent, the situation is that when we know what we want to measure, we can't measure it; where we can measure, we don't know what we have measured.

Possibly my remarks will be taken as indicating that I believe there is some "essence" of value, or that unless one begins with a "neat and tidy" definitive notion of values one cannot inquire further, or that there is one correct notion of value that most inquirers fail to grasp. As emphasized in Chapter I, all these notions are rejected. What I am asserting is that even assuming the most tentative and hypothetical frame of reference, it is frequently so difficult to tell what a given inquirer has measured (and sometimes even what he thought he has measured) that clarification is badly needed.

A comparison between IQ measurement and value measurement may be useful to illustrate some of the issues involved. One criticism of conventional IQ tests is that the aspects of intelligent behavior they measure are so culturally-bound that the tests are unsuitable for subjects with somewhat different cultural backgrounds. For example, some items to be recognized in a test may be much more frequent in middleclass than in lowerclass settings. Some critics also maintain that particular cultural or socioeconomic class values are built into many tests, and individuals coming from other classes or cultures may be penalized when they take the test.

Those who defend the conventional tests often argue that both in ordinary language and in technical psychological language many different uses of 'intelligence' are found, and there is no obligation in any one test to measure all the things to which 'intelligence' might refer (especially since some uses may lead to logical contradictions). And since IQ scores are good predictors of certain types of behavior (such as success in conventional schools), they are useful operationally and little more need be asked of any test. Other defenders take the critics as assuming some "essence" for intelligence that is unscientific, and argue that operationally intelligence is whatever the tests measure.[7]

My view is that in many respects the measurement of intelligence raises issues similar to those found in value measurement, but that the former area is much better developed. In both instances, some type of behavior under investigation is given a label that is used vaguely, inconsistently, and often emotionally in ordinary discourse. But rather than specifying more accurately and clearly what is being measured, inquirers sometimes just leave the impression that measurements are being made of what nearly everyone calls intelligence or value. This almost inevitably gives rise to controversy, for those who advocate some other use for the term than is applicable to the behavior being measured can complain about the invalidity of the measure. Not only may unwary members of the public assume greater significance for given tests than is warranted, but sometimes the investigators

---

[7]For a sampling of the literature in which such controversies appear, see: Kenneth Eells, Allison Davis, Robert S. Havighurst, Virgil E. Herrick, and Ralph Tyler, *Intelligence and Cultural Differences,* Chicago, University of Chicago Press, 1951; Frank Riessman, *The Culturally Deprived Child,* New York, Harper & Row, 1962, Ch. VI; Charles C. Spiker and Boyd R. McCandless, "The Concept of Intelligence and the Philosophy of Science," *Psychological Review,* Vol. 61, 1954; E. G. Boring, *History, Psychology, and Science,* New York, Wiley, 1963, p. 177, pp. 187-189.

themselves (at least in their uncritical moments) similarly inflate what they have done.

In view of the history of the development of IQ tests, there is no mystery as to why they often are good predictors of success in certain school situations. A critic of such school situations may feel that a kind of vicious circle is involved; tests that actually predict success in particular educational contexts, but which are taken as, say, tests of general problem solving ability, may then help bolster what is done in those educational contexts, while the critic believes he has evidence that the educational structures also need reforming. I personally am sympathetic to such criticisms, but even so I think those critics often take as a fundamental defect of IQ tests what is more properly viewed as a limitation. Indeed, as a hypothesis, perhaps one way of grasping what actually is encouraged in many schools would be through a thorough analysis of what behavior on an IQ test leads to a high score.

Moreover, using a broad and encompassing label for a test that actually measures far more restricted types of behavior can be extremely misleading, and possibly for a whole variety of tests a better label could be found. It does not require great acumen to see that when broad labels referring to many different types of behavior are used, considerable controversy is likely to ensue.

This may have social significance when public policy is advocated on the basis of the results of certain tests. For example, Arthur Jensen's recent article, which among many other topics discussed racial differences in intelligence, has created a furor.[8] He mentions extensive and impressive statistical evidence showing that Negroes test on the average about one standard deviation below whites on the average in IQ tests, argues that genetic differences are involved, and suggests that many educational innovations designed to compensate for cultural deprivation have failed because genetic differences rather than environmental differences are involved.

---

[8]Arthur R. Jensen, "How Much Can We Boost IQ and Scholastic Achievement?," *Harvard Educational Review*, Vol. 39, 1969. The next issue (No. 2, Vol. 39) of that journal contains many replies to Jensen.

Some of Jensen's critics focus on his statistical treatments, and of course I am not implying that there are no possible errors in Jensen's work in that respect. However, it would seem foolish to me to doubt that in a great many IQ tests, given under a great many different sets of circumstances, on the average Negroes score considerably lower than whites. The problem then is to ascertain the most appropriate interpretation of such results. One interpretation is that genetic differences are involved. Another is that the tests are unfair to Negroes in terms of the *content* of the tests. Another possibility, which may have important implications beyond the Negro-white issue, concerns not the *content* of the test, but the transactional situations in which the test is given.

For example, some recent work suggests that who gives a test, and with what expectations, may have a marked effect on the results. Robert Rosenthal's work on "experimenter bias" is new enough so that thorough critical assessment is required, but at least *prima facie* his studies in school settings of what happens when teachers are falsely informed there is scientific evidence that some of their students are "spurters" or "bloomers," indicates that the whole set of expectations a teacher has may be far more influential on the results of testing and schooling than is ordinarily assumed. In the study, 20% of the children in a particular elementary school, who were chosen *randomly,* were reported to their teachers as having unusual potential for intellectual growth, on the basis of the results of the impressive sounding *Harvard Test of Inflected Acquisition.* (There is no such test; the children were actually given a standardized, relatively noverbal IQ test.) Eight months later the presumed "bloomers" showed significantly greater gains in IQ than did the remaining children.[9]

A related point is made by Jerome Kagan, who argues that children from some socioeconomic backgrounds, because of their early experiences, often do not "appreciate the nature of a problem" as it is presented to them on IQ tests. He mentions a study

[9] Robert Rosenthal and Lenore Jacobson, *Pygmalion in the Classroom: Teacher Expectation and Pupils' Intellectual Development,* New York, Holt, Rinehart, and Winston, 1968.

212   *The Measurement of Values*

of urban black children in which the IQ distribution had two peaks, one around 60 and the other approximating what is found in white populations. The examiners felt that the very low scores were the result of a failure to appreciate that a test was being given, or of similar factors. He also describes a study (conducted by Francis Palmer) of middle and lower class black Harlem children. In this study the examiners were told not to begin testing any child until the examiner was confident the child was relaxed and understood what was required. This entailed as many as seven hours of rapport sessions before the tests were given. Under those circumstances, it turned out that there were "very few significant differences in mental ability between the lower and middle class populations."[10]

On the basis of a transactional approach to these matters, one indeed would expect that the mutual relations of tester and testee need careful inquiry and may be much more important than often is believed. There is an analogy here between some psychologists and the "fundamentalists" in measurement discussed earlier: both make too sharp a separation between a particular instrument, scale, or formal structure and the use made of it in actual measurements. Even "self-administered" tests are taken in a cultural setting, and both the test and the setting itself may well be perceived differently by people of different backgrounds.

Finally, even assuming that IQ tests do "get at" something more basic and cross-cultural in human behavior than I suspect they do, and fully allowing for the extensive number of measurements that Jensen refers to, the possible influence of what kind of tester is doing the testing (and what expectations he has) should be explored fully and critically before we base public policy on the results found. The large number of converging measurements cited by Jensen may be partly attributable to a frequent repetition of one kind of testing situation for Negro students. Ethnocentrism, subtle or crude, seems such a pervasive characteristic of human behavior that to suspect it may be involved even in controlled testing situations is hardly daring.

10Jerome S. Kagan, "Inadequate Evidence and Illogical Conclusions," *Harvard Educational Review*, Vol. 39, 1969, pp. 275-276.

To avoid misunderstanding, I am not saying there are no group genetic differences in a host of behaviors that might be thought to reflect intelligence. I believe strongly, as does Jensen, that we should not base conclusions about such matters on our ideological convictions. (Some of his critics tend to define 'intelligence' so that *a priori* there can be no significant racial, ethnic, or class differences in IQ.) But equally strongly, I maintain that we should not take for granted the applicability of measures in circumstances different from those in which they were developed, or assume that the measures are more fool-proof than they are. In short, there may be many plausible hypotheses as to why Negroes score lower than whites on IQ tests and often perform less well in school settings that do not require the postulation of genetic differences (assuming we know in the first place who is Negro and who is white). What we need is a full and critical exploration of all those issues.

As yet, nobody seems inclined to base social policy on findings in value measurements, but there do seem to be tendencies to generalize unduly from the findings that have been made. I see no reason at all to doubt, for example, that people who frequently go to church will tend to give a high comparative rating to the word 'salvation' when they are asked to rank-order a list of words, but I also see little reason to take such findings as indicative of great progress in value measurement. Judging generously, in the future as such research is developed perhaps correlations and predictors will emerge that are comparable to those now characteristic of IQ tests. Just as IQ tests are useful for many purposes, so value measurements may be. But until greater clarification is offered of what aspect of behavior is being measured, heated controversies are likely.

E. FINAL COMMENTS

Reflecting on the materials covered in this book, I am optimistic about the possibilities of the measurement of values, but pessimistic about the significance of the results achieved to date. Too often we find that the results which are warranted are relatively trivial, while the more significant and potentially useful results are not evidentially well supported.

Many inquirers seem to assume that some one particular technique of measuring values is generally adequate or can be developed, and yet there are so many uses for the term 'value' that any one mensurational technique would probably be applicable to only some values. A possible remedy is to give up the serious use of 'value' as a broadly inclusive term, and talk only about whatever is in the focus of inquiry at a given moment, such as consumer preferences, or stated likings and dislikings of presented alternatives, or behavioral ideals, or rank-orderings of paintings, etc. Such an approach might well eliminate some relatively pointless controversy and help direct attention to the question of the adequacy of particular measuring techniques for what it is we are trying to measure.

Although I think often clarity would be improved if inquirers were more careful to talk about the particular aspects of behavior they were concerned with in a given inquiry, I believe one reason so many different workers tend to use 'value' to describe the object of their inquiry is that all these investigations are about selective-rejective behavior, and the probability seems high that some generalizations can be found which will apply to all or many forms of that behavior.

The approach suggested here is to focus on valuing transactions as a whole, interpreted as a sequences of selective-rejective adjustive behavior, and then to direct inquiry to the measuring of various important aspects of those transactions, such as the degree of need, the extent to which a particular object will satisfy a particular need, the preferences evinced in the process of restoring equilibria, etc. If that approach were followed, there would be no one measure of value and no one scale of particular or special significance, but rather various aspects of value transactions would be measured in appropriate ways. The measurement of values would be just the measurement of some important aspects of behavior.

This transactional approach would make room for most of the putative objects of measurement mentioned in this book, including the "subjective" and the "unconscious," and would encompass both the preferred and the preferable. Such encompassing would eliminate much of the criticism often encountered when an alleged value measurement is objected to on the ground that it was not value that was measured, but something else.

As discussed in Chapter VIII, on the theory advanced here 'value' is interpreted narrowly in a sense, as the object that satisfies a need. However, all along emphasis was placed on the importance of the whole transaction, and just which aspect of that transaction is most significant will vary according to the purpose of the inquiry. Thus, sometimes we might be more interested in a preference than in a need, or in the need rather than in what would satisfy it. Specifying 'value' in terms of what satisfies a need, then, would not in any way imply that it is more important to measure the value than the other aspects of the transaction.

From this point of view, the specification of the key terms used in describing selective-rejective behavior is often more important than the development of the particular scales used in measuring the phenomena involved. Throughout this book particular and repeated attention therefore has been given to some terminological issues. The main test for resolving those issues is not that proposed by the linguistic analysts so prominent among contemporary Anglo-American philosophers, but the usefulness of the terminology in scientific inquiry.

Viewing value transactions as here suggested requires a demystification of the value field and of the formal side of measurement; if this book has any merit, I hope that it will be along the lines of furthering that demystification. Human behavior is difficult enough to investigate without adding methodogenic problems. Valuing is a pervasive and characteristic form of behavior, and we can expect advances in value measurement as behavioral inquiries advance.

INDEX